READINGS FROM

MY
UTMOST
FOR HIS
HIGHEST®

90 DAYS OF SELECTED
⮞ DEVOTIONALS ⮜

READINGS FROM

MY UTMOST FOR HIS HIGHEST

90 DAYS OF SELECTED
⇒ DEVOTIONALS ⇐

OSWALD CHAMBERS

EDITED BY JAMES REIMANN

Authorized by the Oswald Chambers Publications Association, Ltd.

DISCOVERY HOUSE

PUBLISHERS®

Cover Design: Stan Myers
Interior Design: Steve Gier

United States publication rights are held by
Discovery House Publishers, which is affiliated with
RBC Ministries, Grand Rapids, Michigan.

Requests for permission to quote from this book
should be directed to:
Permissions Department, Discovery House Publishers,
P.O. Box 3566, Grand Rapids, MI 49501.

Unless otherwise indicated, Scripture quotations are from
The New King James Version. © 1979, 1980, 1982,
Thomas Nelson, Inc., Publishers.

ISBN 978-1-57293-385-9

Printed in the United States of America

10 11 12 13 / DP / 7 6 5 4 3 2 1

FOREWORD

With the exception of the Bible, no book has had as profound an effect on my life as *My Utmost for His Highest*. I was introduced to this book years ago, and it has been a part of my daily diet from the first reading.

It was here that God impressed on my heart that precious truth essential to the life of every believer who truly desires to follow Christ: the most important aspect of the Christian life is our personal relationship with Christ.

Few individuals have had the insight into the Person of Christ as Oswald Chambers, and fewer still have been able to make its application so inescapable. This volume is not a treasure to be admired but a message to be lived.

Charles F. Stanley

A Word About
Oswald Chambers

Oswald Chambers was born in Aberdeen, Scotland, on July 24, 1874. When he was fifteen, the family moved to London where Oswald made his public profession of faith in Christ and became a member of Rye Lane Baptist Church. This marked a period of rapid spiritual growth, along with an intense struggle to find God's will and way for his life.

While studying at the University of Edinburgh (1895–96), he experienced a major redirection in life and decided to train for the Christian ministry. He left the university and entered Dunoon College, near Glasgow, where he spent nine years, first as a theological student, then as a tutor of philosophy. Under the wise guidance of Rev. Duncan MacGregor, his mentor and friend, Oswald matured greatly and came through a long "dark night of the soul" into a deeper and more joyful knowledge of Christ.

In 1906 and 1907 Oswald spent six months teaching at God's Bible School in Cincinnati, Ohio. From there he went to Japan, visiting the Tokyo Bible School, founded by Charles and Lettie Cowman. While serving as a travelling speaker and representative of the League of Prayer in Britain, Oswald met Gertrude Hobbs. Their friendship blossomed during a voyage to the United States in the summer of 1908, and two years later they were married. Oswald called her "Beloved Disciple," shortened to the initials B.D., and spoken as "Biddy." For the rest of her life, she was known by this affectionate nickname. Their only child, Kathleen, was born in May 1913.

A long-time dream of Oswald's became reality in January 1911 with the opening of the Bible Training College (BTC) near Clapham

Common in London, where he served as Principal and main teacher. During Oswald's lectures Biddy sat in the back of the room recording his words verbatim in her precise Pittman's shorthand. Trained as a court stenographer, she could take dictation rapidly while remaining engaged with her husband's purpose as he taught.

The outbreak of World War I in August 1914 led to the closing of the BTC within a year. Oswald volunteered as a YMCA secretary in Egypt, where Biddy, Kathleen, and several former students from the BTC joined him to assist in the work. At Zeitoun Camp, near Cairo, Oswald quickly established himself as a friend of the troops and a man of uncommon spiritual insight.

In late October 1917 Oswald underwent an emergency appendectomy and appeared to be recovering. But two weeks later, while still in hospital, he suffered a relapse and died early in the morning on November 15. He was forty-three years old.

For the next two years, Biddy and Kathleen continued to work among the troops at Zeitoun. Gradually it became clear to Biddy that her calling in life was to give her husband's words to the world. In so doing, she continued the dream she and Oswald had shared of working together to help others. Upon her return to England in 1919, Biddy continued transcribing her shorthand notes and preparing them for publication.

While maintaining a boarding house for students in Oxford, Biddy compiled a book of daily readings which she titled *My Utmost for His Highest*. Since it was first published in 1927, *My Utmost* has been continuously in print and has sold millions of copies. It exists today in more than forty different languages, and every day, multiplied thousands of people around the world open its pages seeking a word from the Lord through His servant Oswald Chambers.

David McCasland

LET US KEEP TO THE POINT

". . . my earnest expectation and hope that in nothing I shall be ashamed, but with all boldness, as always, so now also Christ will be magnified in my body, whether by life or by death"
(PHILIPPIANS 1:20).

My Utmost for His Highest. ". . . my earnest expectation and hope that in nothing I shall be ashamed . . . ." We will all feel very much ashamed if we do not yield to Jesus the areas of our lives He has asked us to yield to Him. It's as if Paul were saying, "My determined purpose is to be my utmost for His highest—my best for His glory." To reach that level of determination is a matter of the will, not of debate or of reasoning. It is absolute and irrevocable surrender of the will at that point. An undue amount of thought and consideration for ourselves is what keeps us from making that decision, although we cover it up with the pretense that it is others we are considering. When we think seriously about what it will cost others if we obey the call of Jesus, we tell God He doesn't know what our obedience will mean. Keep to the point—He does know. Shut out every other thought and keep yourself before God in this one thing only—my utmost for His highest. I am determined to be absolutely and entirely for Him and Him alone.

My Unstoppable Determination for His Holiness. "Whether it means life or death—it makes no difference!" (see 1:21). Paul was determined that nothing would stop him from doing exactly what God wanted. But before we choose to follow God's will, a crisis must develop in our lives. This happens because we tend to be unresponsive to God's gentler nudges. He brings us to the place where He asks us to be our utmost for Him and we begin to debate. He then providentially produces a crisis where we have to decide—for or against. That moment becomes a great crossroads in our lives. If a crisis has come to you on any front, surrender your will to Jesus absolutely and irrevocably.

WILL YOU GO OUT WITHOUT KNOWING?

"He went out, not knowing where he was going" (HEBREWS 11:8).

Have you ever "gone out" in this way? If so, there is no logical answer possible when anyone asks you what you are doing. One of the most difficult questions to answer in Christian work is, "What do you expect to do?" You don't know what you are going to do. The only thing you know is that God knows what He is doing. Continually examine your attitude toward God to see if you are willing to "go out" in every area of your life, trusting in God entirely. It is this attitude that keeps you in constant wonder, because you don't know what God is going to do next. Each morning as you wake, there is a new opportunity to "go out," building your confidence in God. ". . . do not worry about your life . . . nor about the body . . ." (Luke 12:22). In other words, don't worry about the things that concerned you before you did "go out."

Have you been asking God what He is going to do? He will never tell you. God does not tell you what He is going to do—He reveals to you who He is. Do you believe in a miracle-working God, and will you "go out" in complete surrender to Him until you are not surprised one iota by anything He does?

Believe God is always the God you know Him to be when you are nearest to Him. Then think how unnecessary and disrespectful worry is! Let the attitude of your life be a continual willingness to "go out" in dependence upon God, and your life will have a sacred and inexpressible charm about it that is very satisfying to Jesus. You must learn to "go out" through your convictions, creeds, or experiences until you come to the point in your faith where there is nothing between yourself and God.

"CLOUDS AND DARKNESS"

"Clouds and darkness surround Him . . ." (PSALM 97:2).

A person who has not been born again by the Spirit of God will tell you that the teachings of Jesus are simple. But when he is baptized by the Holy Spirit, he finds that "clouds and darkness surround Him . . . ." When we come into close contact with the teachings of Jesus Christ we have our first realization of this. The only possible way to have full understanding of the teachings of Jesus is through the light of the Spirit of God shining inside us. If we have never had the experience of taking our casual, religious shoes off our casual, religious feet—getting rid of all the excessive informality with which we approach God—it is questionable whether we have ever stood in His presence. The people who are flippant and disrespectful in their approach to God are those who have never been introduced to Jesus Christ. Only after the amazing delight and liberty of realizing what Jesus Christ does, comes the impenetrable "darkness" of realizing who He is.

Jesus said, "The words that I speak to you are spirit, and they are life" (John 6:63). Once, the Bible was just so many words to us—"clouds and darkness"—then, suddenly, the words become spirit and life because Jesus re-speaks them to us when our circumstances make the words new. That is the way God speaks to us; not by visions and dreams, but by words. When a man gets to God, it is by the most simple way—words.

"Why Can I Not Follow You Now?"

"Peter said to Him, 'Lord, why can I not follow You now?' "
(John 13:37).

There are times when you can't understand why you cannot do what you want to do. When God brings a time of waiting, and appears to be unresponsive, don't fill it with busyness, just wait. The time of waiting may come to teach you the meaning of sanctification—to be set apart from sin and made holy—or it may come after the process of sanctification has begun to teach you what service means. Never run before God gives you His direction. If you have the slightest doubt, then He is not guiding. Whenever there is doubt—wait.

At first you may see clearly what God's will is—the severance of a friendship, the breaking off of a business relationship, or something else you feel is distinctly God's will for you to do. But never act on the impulse of that feeling. If you do, you will cause difficult situations to arise which will take years to untangle. Wait for God's timing and He will do it without any heartache or disappointment. When it is a question of the providential will of God, wait for God to move.

Peter did not wait for God. He predicted in his own mind where the test would come, and it came where he did not expect it. "I will lay down my life for Your sake." Peter's statement was honest but ignorant. "Jesus answered him, ' . . . the rooster shall not crow till you have denied Me three times' " (13:38). This was said with a deeper knowledge of Peter than Peter had of himself. He could not follow Jesus because he did not know himself or his own capabilities well enough. Natural devotion may be enough to attract us to Jesus, to make us feel His irresistible charm, but it will never make us disciples. Natural devotion will deny Jesus, always falling short of what it means to truly follow Him.

THE LIFE OF POWER TO FOLLOW

**"Jesus answered him, 'Where I am going you cannot follow Me
now, but you shall follow Me afterward' "**
(JOHN 13:36).

And when He had spoken this, He said to him, 'Follow Me' " (John
21:19). Three years earlier Jesus had said, "Follow Me" (Matthew 4:19),
and Peter followed with no hesitation. The irresistible attraction
of Jesus was upon him and he did not need the Holy Spirit to help him do
it. Later he came to the place where he denied Jesus, and his heart broke.
Then he received the Holy Spirit and Jesus said again, "Follow Me" (John
21:19). Now no one is in front of Peter except the Lord Jesus Christ. The
first "Follow Me" was nothing mysterious; it was an external following.
Jesus is now asking for an internal sacrifice and yielding (see 21:18).

Between these two times Peter denied Jesus with oaths and curses
(see Matthew 26:69–75). But then he came completely to the end of
himself and all of his self-sufficiency. There was no part of himself he
would ever rely on again. In his state of destitution, he was finally ready
to receive all that the risen Lord had for him. ". . . He breathed on them,
and said to them, 'Receive the Holy Spirit' " (John 20:22). No matter
what changes God has performed in you, never rely on them. Build only
on a Person, the Lord Jesus Christ, and on the Spirit He gives.

All our promises and resolutions end in denial because we have no
power to accomplish them. When we come to the end of ourselves, not
just mentally but completely, we are able to "receive the Holy Spirit."
"Receive the Holy Spirit"—the idea is that of invasion. There is now only
One who directs the course of your life, the Lord Jesus Christ.

WORSHIP

**"He moved from there to the mountain east of Bethel,
and he pitched his tent with Bethel on the west
and Ai on the east; there he built an altar to the LORD
and called on the name of the LORD"**
(GENESIS 12:8).

Worship is giving God the best that He has given you. Be careful what you do with the best you have. Whenever you get a blessing from God, give it back to Him as a love-gift. Take time to meditate before God and offer the blessing back to Him in a deliberate act of worship. If you hoard it for yourself, it will turn into spiritual dry rot, as the manna did when it was hoarded (see Exodus 16:20). God will never allow you to keep a spiritual blessing completely for yourself. It must be given back to Him so that He can make it a blessing to others.

Bethel is the symbol of fellowship with God; Ai is the symbol of the world. Abram "pitched his tent" between the two. The lasting value of our public service for God is measured by the depth of the intimacy of our private times of fellowship and oneness with Him. Rushing in and out of worship is wrong every time—there is always plenty of time to worship God. Days set apart for quiet can be a trap, detracting from the need to have daily quiet time with God. That is why we must "pitch our tents" where we will always have quiet times with Him, however noisy our times with the world may be. There are not three levels of spiritual life—worship, waiting, and work. Yet some of us seem to jump like spiritual frogs from worship to waiting, and from waiting to work. God's idea is that the three should go together as one. They were always together in the life of our Lord and in perfect harmony. It is a discipline that must be developed; it will not happen overnight.

INTIMATE WITH JESUS

"Jesus said to him, 'Have I been with you so long, and yet you have not known Me, Philip?'"
(JOHN 14:9).

These words were not spoken as a rebuke, nor even with surprise; Jesus was encouraging Philip to draw closer. Yet the last person we get intimate with is Jesus. Before Pentecost the disciples knew Jesus as the One who gave them power to conquer demons and to bring about a revival (see Luke 10:18-20). It was a wonderful intimacy, but there was a much closer intimacy to come: ". . . I have called you friends . . ." (John 15:15). True friendship is rare on earth. It means identifying with someone in thought, heart, and spirit. The whole experience of life is designed to enable us to enter into this closest relationship with Jesus Christ. We receive His blessings and know His Word, but do we really know Him?

Jesus said, "It is to your advantage that I go away . . ." (John 16:7). He left that relationship to lead them even closer. It is a joy to Jesus when a disciple takes time to walk more intimately with Him. The bearing of fruit is always shown in Scripture to be the visible result of an intimate relationship with Jesus Christ (see John 15:1-4).

Once we get intimate with Jesus we are never lonely and we never lack for understanding or compassion. We can continually pour out our hearts to Him without being perceived as overly emotional or pitiful. The Christian who is truly intimate with Jesus will never draw attention to himself but will only show the evidence of a life where Jesus is completely in control. This is the outcome of allowing Jesus to satisfy every area of life to its depth. The picture resulting from such a life is that of the strong, calm balance that our Lord gives to those who are intimate with Him.

IS MY SACRIFICE LIVING?

**"Abraham built an altar . . . ; and he bound Isaac his son
and laid him on the altar . . ."**
(GENESIS 22:9).

This event is a picture of the mistake we make in thinking that the ultimate God wants of us is the sacrifice of death. What God wants is the sacrifice *through* death which enables us to do what Jesus did, that is, sacrifice our lives. Not—"Lord, I am ready to go with You . . . to death" (Luke 22:33). But—"I am willing to be identified with Your death so that I may sacrifice my life to God."

We seem to think that God wants us to give up things! God purified Abraham from this error, and the same process is at work in our lives. God never tells us to give up things just for the sake of giving them up, but He tells us to give them up for the sake of the only thing worth having, namely, life with Himself. It is a matter of loosening the bands that hold back our lives. Those bands are loosened immediately by identification with the death of Jesus. Then we enter into a relationship with God whereby we may sacrifice our lives to Him.

It is of no value to God to give Him your life for death. He wants you to be a *"living* sacrifice"—to let Him have all your strengths that have been saved and sanctified through Jesus (Romans 12:1). This is what is acceptable to God.

PRAYERFUL INNER-SEARCHING

"May your whole spirit, soul, and body be preserved blameless . . ."
(1 THESSALONIANS 5:23).

Your whole spirit . . . ." The great, mysterious work of the Holy Spirit is in the deep recesses of our being which we cannot reach. Read Psalm 139. The psalmist implies—"O Lord, You are the God of the early mornings, the God of the late nights, the God of the mountain peaks, and the God of the sea. But, my God, my soul has horizons further away than those of early mornings, deeper darkness than the nights of earth, higher peaks than any mountain peaks, greater depths than any sea in nature. You who are the God of all these, be my God. I cannot reach to the heights or to the depths; there are motives I cannot discover, dreams I cannot realize. My God, search me."

Do we believe that God can fortify and protect our thought processes far beyond where we can go? ". . . *the blood of Jesus Christ His Son cleanses us from all sin*" (1 John 1:7). If this verse means cleansing only on our conscious level, may God have mercy on us. The man who has been dulled by sin will say that he is not even conscious of it. But the cleansing from sin we experience will reach to the heights and depths of our spirit if we will "walk in the light as He is in the light" (1:7). The same Spirit that fed the life of Jesus Christ will feed the life of our spirit. It is only when we are protected by God with the miraculous sacredness of the Holy Spirit that our spirit, soul, and body can be preserved in pure uprightness until the coming of Jesus—no longer condemned in God's sight.

We should more frequently allow our minds to meditate on these great, massive truths of God.

THE FAITH TO PERSEVERE

"Because you have kept My command to persevere . . ."
(REVELATION 3:10).

Perseverance means more than endurance—more than simply holding on until the end. A saint's life is in the hands of God like a bow and arrow in the hands of an archer. God is aiming at something the saint cannot see, but our Lord continues to stretch and strain, and every once in a while the saint says, "I can't take any more." Yet God pays no attention; He goes on stretching until His purpose is in sight, and then He lets the arrow fly. Entrust yourself to God's hands. Is there something in your life for which you need perseverance right now? Maintain your intimate relationship with Jesus Christ through the perseverance of faith. Proclaim as Job did, "Though He slay me, yet will I trust Him" (Job 13:15).

Faith is not some weak and pitiful emotion, but is strong and vigorous confidence built on the fact that God is holy love. And even though you cannot see Him right now and cannot understand what He is doing, you know *Him*. Disaster occurs in your life when you lack the mental composure that comes from establishing yourself on the eternal truth that God is holy love. Faith is the supreme effort of your life—throwing yourself with abandon and total confidence upon God.

God ventured His all in Jesus Christ to save us, and now He wants us to venture our all with total abandoned confidence in Him. There are areas in our lives where that faith has not worked in us as yet—places still untouched by the life of God. There were none of those places in Jesus Christ's life, and there are to be none in ours. Jesus prayed, "This is eternal life, that they may know You . . ." (John 17:3). The real meaning of eternal life is a life that can face anything it has to face without wavering. If we will take this view, life will become one great romance—a glorious opportunity of seeing wonderful things all the time. God is disciplining us to get us into this central place of power.

WHAT MY OBEDIENCE TO GOD COSTS OTHER PEOPLE

"As they led Him away, they laid hold of a certain man, Simon . . . , and on him they laid the cross that he might bear it after Jesus"
(LUKE 23:26).

If we obey God, it is going to cost other people more than it costs us, and that is where the pain begins. If we are in love with our Lord, obedience does not cost us anything—it is a delight. But to those who do not love Him, our obedience does cost a great deal. If we obey God, it will mean that other people's plans are upset. They will ridicule us as if to say, "You call this Christianity?" We could prevent the suffering, but not if we are obedient to God. We must let the cost be paid.

When our obedience begins to cost others, our human pride entrenches itself and we say, "I will never accept anything from anyone." But we must, or disobey God. We have no right to think that the type of relationships we have with others should be any different from those the Lord Himself had (see Luke 8:1–3).

A lack of progress in our spiritual life results when we try to bear all the costs ourselves. And actually, we cannot. Because we are so involved in the universal purposes of God, others are immediately affected by our obedience to Him. Will we remain faithful in our obedience to God and be willing to suffer the humiliation of refusing to be independent? Or will we do just the opposite and say, "I will not cause other people to suffer"? We can disobey God if we choose, and it will bring immediate relief to the situation, but it will grieve our Lord. If, however, we obey God, He will care for those who have suffered the consequences of our obedience. We must simply obey and leave all the consequences with Him.

Beware of the inclination to dictate to God what consequences you would allow as a condition of your obedience to Him.

HAVE YOU EVER BEEN ALONE WITH GOD?

"When they were alone, He explained all things to His disciples"
(MARK 4:34).

OUR SOLITUDE WITH HIM. Jesus doesn't take us aside and explain things to us all the time; He explains things to us as we are able to understand them. The lives of others are examples for us, but God requires us to examine our own souls. It is slow work—so slow that it takes God all of time and eternity to make a man or woman conform to His purpose. We can only be used by God after we allow Him to show us the deep, hidden areas of our own character. It is astounding how ignorant we are about ourselves! We don't even recognize the envy, laziness, or pride within us when we see it. But Jesus will reveal to us everything we have held within ourselves before His grace began to work. How many of us have learned to look inwardly with courage?

We have to get rid of the idea that we understand ourselves. That is always the last bit of pride to go. The only One who understands us is God. The greatest curse in our spiritual life is pride. If we have ever had a glimpse of what we are like in the sight of God, we will never say, "Oh, I'm so unworthy." We will understand that this goes without saying. But as long as there is any doubt that we are unworthy, God will continue to close us in until He gets us alone. Whenever there is any element of pride or conceit remaining, Jesus can't teach us anything. He will allow us to experience heartbreak or the disappointment we feel when our intellectual pride is wounded. He will reveal numerous misplaced affections or desires—things over which we never thought He would have to get us alone. Many things are shown to us, often without effect. But when God gets us alone over them, they will be clear.

HAVE YOU EVER BEEN ALONE WITH GOD?

"When He was alone . . . the twelve asked Him about the parable"
(MARK 4:10).

HIS SOLITUDE WITH US. When God gets us alone through suffering, heartbreak, temptation, disappointment, sickness, or by thwarted desires, a broken friendship, or a new friendship—when He gets us absolutely alone, and we are totally speechless, unable to ask even one question, then He begins to teach us. Notice Jesus Christ's training of the Twelve. It was the disciples, not the crowd outside, who were confused. His disciples constantly asked Him questions, and He constantly explained things to them, but they didn't understand until after they received the Holy Spirit (see John 14:26).

As you journey with God, the only thing He intends to be clear is the way He deals with your soul. The sorrows and difficulties in the lives of others will be absolutely confusing to you. We think we understand another person's struggle until God reveals the same shortcomings in our lives. There are vast areas of stubbornness and ignorance the Holy Spirit has to reveal in each of us, but it can only be done when Jesus gets us alone.

Are we alone with Him now? Or are we more concerned with our own ideas, friendships, and cares for our bodies? Jesus cannot teach us anything until we quiet all our intellectual questions and get alone with Him.

CALLED BY GOD

**"I heard the voice of the Lord, saying: 'Whom shall I send,
and who will go for Us?' Then I said, 'Here am I! Send me' "**
(ISAIAH 6:8).

God did not direct His call to Isaiah—Isaiah overheard God saying,
". . . who will go for Us?" The call of God is not just for a select
few but for everyone. Whether I hear God's call or not depends
on the condition of my ears, and exactly what I hear depends upon my
spiritual attitude. "Many are called, but few are chosen" (Matthew 22:14).
That is, few prove that they are the chosen ones. The chosen ones are
those who have come into a relationship with God through Jesus Christ
and have had their spiritual condition changed and their ears opened.
Then they hear "the voice of the Lord" continually asking, ". . . who will
go for Us?" However, God doesn't single out someone and say, "Now,
you go." He did not force His will on Isaiah. Isaiah was in the presence
of God, and he overheard the call. His response, performed in complete
freedom, could only be to say, "Here am I! Send me."

Remove the thought from your mind of expecting God to come to
force you or to plead with you. When our Lord called His disciples, He did
it without irresistible pressure from the outside. The quiet, yet passionate,
insistence of His "Follow Me" was spoken to men whose every sense was
receptive (Matthew 4:19). If we will allow the Holy Spirit to bring us face to
face with God, we too will hear what Isaiah heard—"the voice of the Lord."
In perfect freedom we too will say, "Here am I! Send me."

IS YOUR ABILITY TO
SEE GOD BLINDED?

"Lift up your eyes on high, and see who has created these things . . ."
(ISAIAH 40:26).

The people of God in Isaiah's time had starved their imagination by looking on the face of idols. But Isaiah made them look up at the heavens; that is, he made them begin to use their imagination correctly. If we are children of God, we have a tremendous treasure in nature and will realize that it is holy and sacred. We will see God reaching out to us in every wind that blows, every sunrise and sunset, every cloud in the sky, every flower that blooms, and every leaf that fades, if we will only begin to use our starved imagination to visualize it.

The real test of spiritual focus is being able to bring your thoughts and imagination under control. Is your mind focused on the face of an idol? Is the idol yourself? Is it your work? Is it your idea of what a servant should be, or maybe your experience of salvation and sanctification? If so, then your ability to see God is blinded. You will be powerless when faced with difficulties and will be forced to endure in darkness. If your power to see has been blinded, don't look back on your own experiences, but look to God. It is God you need. Go beyond yourself and away from the faces of your idols and away from everything else that has been blinding your thinking, your imagination. Wake up and accept the ridicule that Isaiah gave to his people, and deliberately turn your thoughts and your eyes to God.

One of the reasons for our sense of futility in prayer is that we have lost our power to visualize. We can no longer even imagine putting ourselves deliberately before God. It is actually more important to be broken bread and poured-out wine in the area of intercession than in our personal contact with others. The power of imagination is what God gives a saint so that he can go beyond himself and be firmly placed into relationships he never before experienced.

IS YOUR MIND STAYED ON GOD?

"You will keep him in perfect peace, whose mind is stayed on You, because he trusts in You"
(ISAIAH 26:3).

I s your mind stayed on God or is it starved? Starvation of the mind, caused by neglect, is one of the chief sources of exhaustion and weakness in a servant's life. If you have never used your mind to place yourself before God, begin to do it now. There is no reason to wait for God to come to you. You must turn your thoughts and your eyes away from the face of idols and look to Him and be saved (see Isaiah 45:22).

Your creative mind is the greatest gift God has given you and it ought to be devoted entirely to Him. You should seek to be "bringing every thought into captivity to the obedience of Christ . . ." (2 Corinthians 10:5). This will be one of the greatest assets of your faith when a time of trial comes, because then your faith and the Spirit of God will work together. When you have thoughts and ideas that are worthy of credit to God, learn to compare and associate them with all that happens in nature—the rising and the setting of the sun, the shining of the moon and the stars, and the changing of the seasons. You will begin to see that your thoughts are from God as well, and your mind will no longer be at the mercy of your impulsive thinking, but will always be used in service to God.

"We have sinned with our fathers . . . [and] . . . did not remember . . ." (Psalm 106:6–7). Then prod your memory and wake up immediately. Don't say to yourself, "But God is not talking to me right now." He ought to be. Remember whose you are and whom you serve. Encourage yourself to remember, and your affection for God will increase tenfold. Your mind will no longer be starved, but will be quick and enthusiastic, and your hope will be inexpressibly bright.

ARE YOU LISTENING TO GOD?

**"They said to Moses, 'You speak with us, and we will hear;
but let not God speak with us, lest we die' "**
(EXODUS 20:19).

We don't consciously and deliberately disobey God—we simply don't listen to Him. God has given His commands to us, but we pay no attention to them—not because of willful disobedience, but because we do not truly love and respect Him. "If you love Me, keep My commandments" (John 14:15). Once we realize we have constantly been showing disrespect to God, we will be filled with shame and humiliation for ignoring Him.

"You speak with us, . . . but let not God speak with us . . . ." We show how little love we have for God by preferring to listen to His servants rather than to Him. We like to listen to personal testimonies, but we don't want God Himself to speak to us. Why are we so terrified for God to speak to us? It is because we know that when God speaks we must either do what He asks or tell Him we will not obey. But if it is simply one of God's servants speaking to us, we feel obedience is optional, not imperative. We respond by saying, "Well, that's only your own idea, even though I don't deny that what you said is probably God's truth."

Am I constantly humiliating God by ignoring Him, while He lovingly continues to treat me as His child? Once I finally do hear Him, the humiliation I have heaped on Him returns to me. My response then becomes, "Lord, why was I so insensitive and obstinate?" This is always the result once we hear God. But our real delight in finally hearing Him is tempered with the shame we feel for having taken so long to do so.

THE DEVOTION OF HEARING

"Samuel answered, 'Speak, for Your servant hears' "
(1 SAMUEL 3:10).

Just because I have listened carefully and intently to one thing from God does not mean that I will listen to everything He says. I show God my lack of love and respect for Him by the insensitivity of my heart and mind toward what He says. If I love my friend, I will instinctively understand what he wants. And Jesus said, "You are My friends . . ." (John 15:14). Have I disobeyed some command of my Lord's this week? If I had realized that it was a command of Jesus, I would not have deliberately disobeyed it. But most of us show incredible disrespect to God because we don't even hear Him. He might as well never have spoken to us.

The goal of my spiritual life is such close identification with Jesus Christ that I will always hear God and know that God always hears me (see John 11:41). If I am united with Jesus Christ, I hear God all the time through the devotion of hearing. A flower, a tree, or a servant of God may convey God's message to me. What hinders me from hearing is my attention to other things. It is not that I don't want to hear God, but I am not devoted in the right areas of my life. I am devoted to things and even to service and my own convictions. God may say whatever He wants, but I just don't hear Him. The attitude of a child of God should always be, "Speak, for Your servant hears." If I have not developed and nurtured this devotion of hearing, I can only hear God's voice at certain times. At other times I become deaf to Him because my attention is to other things—things which I think I must do. This is not living the life of a child of God. Have you heard God's voice today?

THE DISCIPLINE OF HEARING

"Whatever I tell you in the dark, speak in the light; and what you hear in the ear, preach on the housetops"
(MATTHEW 10:27).

Sometimes God puts us through the experience and discipline of darkness to teach us to hear and obey Him. Song birds are taught to sing in the dark, and God puts us into "the shadow of His hand" until we learn to hear Him (Isaiah 49:2). "Whatever I tell you in the dark. . ."—pay attention when God puts you into darkness, and keep your mouth closed while you are there. Are you in the dark right now in your circumstances, or in your life with God? If so, then remain quiet. If you open your mouth in the dark, you will speak while in the wrong mood—darkness is the time to listen. Don't talk to other people about it; don't read books to find out the reason for the darkness; just listen and obey. If you talk to other people, you cannot hear what God is saying. When you are in the dark, listen, and God will give you a very precious message for someone else once you are back in the light.

After every time of darkness, we should experience a mixture of delight and humiliation. If there is only delight, I question whether we have really heard God at all. We should experience delight for having heard God speak, but mostly humiliation for having taken so long to hear Him! Then we will exclaim, "How slow I have been to listen and understand what God has been telling me!" And yet God has been saying it for days and even weeks. But once you hear Him, He gives you the gift of humiliation, which brings a softness of heart—a gift that will always cause you to listen to God *now*.

"AM I MY BROTHER'S KEEPER?"

"None of us lives to himself . . ."
(ROMANS 14:7).

Has it ever dawned on you that you are responsible spiritually to God for other people? For instance, if I allow any turning away from God in my private life, everyone around me suffers. We "sit *together* in the heavenly places . . ." (Ephesians 2:6). "If one member suffers, all the members suffer with it . . ." (1 Corinthians 12:26). If you allow physical selfishness, mental carelessness, moral insensitivity, or spiritual weakness, everyone in contact with you will suffer. But you ask, "Who is sufficient to be able to live up to such a lofty standard?" "Our sufficiency is from God . . ." and God alone (2 Corinthians 3:5).

"You shall be witnesses to Me . . ." (Acts 1:8). How many of us are willing to spend every bit of our nervous, mental, moral, and spiritual energy for Jesus Christ? That is what God means when He uses the word witness. But it takes time, so be patient with yourself. Why has God left us on the earth? Is it simply to be saved and sanctified? No, it is to be at work in service to Him. Am I willing to be broken bread and poured-out wine for Him? Am I willing to be of no value to this age or this life except for one purpose and one alone—to be used to disciple men and women to the Lord Jesus Christ? My life of service to God is the way I say "thank you" to Him for His inexpressibly wonderful salvation. Remember, it is quite possible for God to set any of us aside if we refuse to be of service to Him—". . . lest, when I have preached to others, I myself should become disqualified" (1 Corinthians 9:27).

THE INSPIRATION OF SPIRITUAL INITIATIVE

"Arise from the dead . . ."
(EPHESIANS 5:14).

Not all initiative, the willingness to take the first step, is inspired by God. Someone may say to you, "Get up and get going! Take your reluctance by the throat and throw it overboard—just do what needs to be done!" That is what we mean by ordinary human initiative. But when the Spirit of God comes to us and says, in effect, "Get up and get going," suddenly we find that the initiative is inspired.

We all have many dreams and aspirations when we are young, but sooner or later we realize we have no power to accomplish them. We cannot do the things we long to do, so our tendency is to think of our dreams and aspirations as dead. But God comes and says to us, "Arise from the dead . . . ." When God sends His inspiration, it comes to us with such miraculous power that we are able to "arise from the dead" and do the impossible. The remarkable thing about spiritual initiative is that the life and power comes after we "get up and get going." God does not give us overcoming life—He gives us life *as we overcome*. When the inspiration of God comes, and He says, "Arise from the dead . . . ," we have to get ourselves up; God will not lift us up. Our Lord said to the man with the withered hand, "Stretch out your hand" (Matthew 12:13). As soon as the man did so, his hand was healed. But he had to take the initiative. If we will take the initiative to overcome, we will find that we have the inspiration of God, because He immediately gives us the power of life.

TAKING THE INITIATIVE
AGAINST DEPRESSION

"Arise and eat"
(1 KINGS 19:5).

The angel in this passage did not give Elijah a vision, or explain the Scriptures to him, or do anything remarkable. He simply told Elijah to do a very ordinary thing, that is, to get up and eat. If we were never depressed, we would not be alive—only material things don't suffer depression. If human beings were not capable of depression, we would have no capacity for happiness and exaltation. There are things in life that are designed to depress us; for example, things that are associated with death. Whenever you examine yourself, always take into account your capacity for depression.

When the Spirit of God comes to us, He does not give us glorious visions, but He tells us to do the most ordinary things imaginable. Depression tends to turn us away from the everyday things of God's creation. But whenever God steps in, His inspiration is to do the most natural, simple things—things we would never have imagined God was in, but as we do them we find Him there. The inspiration that comes to us in this way is an initiative against depression. But we must take the first step and do it in the inspiration of God. If, however, we do something simply to overcome our depression, we will only deepen it. But when the Spirit of God leads us instinctively to do something, the moment we do it the depression is gone. As soon as we arise and obey, we enter a higher plane of life.

TAKING THE INITIATIVE AGAINST DESPAIR

"Rise, let us be going"
(MATTHEW 26:46).

In the Garden of Gethsemane, the disciples went to sleep when they should have stayed awake, and once they realized what they had done it produced despair. The sense of having done something irreversible tends to make us despair. We say, "Well, it's all over and ruined now; what's the point in trying anymore." If we think this kind of despair is an exception, we are mistaken. It is a very ordinary human experience. Whenever we realize we have not taken advantage of a magnificent opportunity, we are apt to sink into despair. But Jesus comes and lovingly says to us, in essence, "Sleep on now. That opportunity is lost forever and you can't change that. But get up, and let's go on to the next thing." In other words, let the past sleep, but let it sleep in the sweet embrace of Christ, and let us go on into the invincible future with Him.

There will be experiences like this in each of our lives. We will have times of despair caused by real events in our lives, and we will be unable to lift ourselves out of them. The disciples, in this instance, had done a downright unthinkable thing—they had gone to sleep instead of watching with Jesus. But our Lord came to them taking the spiritual initiative against their despair and said, in effect, "Get up, and do the next thing." If we are inspired by God, what is the next thing? It is to trust Him absolutely and to pray on the basis of His redemption.

Never let the sense of past failure defeat your next step.

TAKING THE INITIATIVE AGAINST DRUDGERY

"Arise, shine . . ."
(ISAIAH 60:1).

When it comes to taking the initiative against drudgery, we have to take the first step as though there were no God. There is no point in waiting for God to help us—He will not. But once we arise, immediately we find He is there. Whenever God gives us His inspiration, suddenly taking the initiative becomes a moral issue—a matter of obedience. Then we must act to be obedient and not continue to lie down doing nothing. If we will arise and shine, drudgery will be divinely transformed.

Drudgery is one of the finest tests to determine the genuineness of our character. Drudgery is work that is far removed from anything we think of as ideal work. It is the utterly hard, menial, tiresome, and dirty work. And when we experience it, our spirituality is instantly tested and we will know whether or not we are spiritually genuine. Read John 13. In this chapter, we see the Incarnate God performing the greatest example of drudgery—washing fishermen's feet. He then says to them, "If I then, your Lord and Teacher, have washed your feet, you also ought to wash one another's feet" (John 13:14). The inspiration of God is required if drudgery is to shine with the light of God upon it. In some cases the way a person does a task makes that work sanctified and holy forever. It may be a very common everyday task, but after we have seen it done, it becomes different. When the Lord does something through us, He always transforms it. Our Lord takes our human flesh and transforms it, and now every believer's body has become "the temple of the Holy Spirit" (1 Corinthians 6:19).

TAKING THE INITIATIVE AGAINST DAYDREAMING

"Arise, let us go from here"
(JOHN 14:31).

Daydreaming about something in order to do it properly is right, but daydreaming about it when we should be doing it is wrong. In this passage, after having said these wonderful things to His disciples, we might have expected our Lord to tell them to go away and meditate over them all. But Jesus never allowed idle daydreaming. When our purpose is to seek God and to discover His will for us, daydreaming is right and acceptable. But when our inclination is to spend time daydreaming over what we have already been told to do, it is unacceptable and God's blessing is never on it. God will take the initiative against this kind of daydreaming by prodding us to action. His instructions to us will be along the lines of this: "Don't sit or stand there, just go!"

If we are quietly waiting before God after He has said to us, "Come aside by yourselves . . ." then that is meditation before Him to seek His will (Mark 6:31). Beware, however, of giving in to mere daydreaming once God has spoken. Allow Him to be the source of all your dreams, joys, and delights, and be careful to go and obey what He has said. If you are in love with someone, you don't sit and daydream about that person all the time—you go and do something for him. That is what Jesus Christ expects us to do. Daydreaming after God has spoken is an indication that we do not trust Him.

DO YOU REALLY LOVE HIM?

"She has done a good work for Me"
(MARK 14:6).

If what we call love doesn't take us beyond ourselves, it is not really love. If we have the idea that love is characterized as cautious, wise, sensible, shrewd, and never taken to extremes, we have missed the true meaning. This may describe affection and it may bring us a warm feeling, but it is not a true and accurate description of love.

Have you ever been driven to do something for God not because you felt that it was useful or your duty to do so, or that there was anything in it for you, but simply because you love Him? Have you ever realized that you can give things to God that are of value to Him? Or are you just sitting around daydreaming about the greatness of His redemption, while neglecting all the things you could be doing for Him? I'm not referring to works which could be regarded as divine and miraculous, but ordinary, simple human things—things which would be evidence to God that you are totally surrendered to Him. Have you ever created what Mary of Bethany created in the heart of the Lord Jesus? "She has done a good work for Me."

There are times when it seems as if God watches to see if we will give Him even small gifts of surrender, just to show how genuine our love is for Him. To be surrendered to God is of more value than our personal holiness. Concern over our personal holiness causes us to focus our eyes on ourselves, and we become overly concerned about the way we walk and talk and look, out of fear of offending God. ". . . but perfect love casts out fear . . ." once we are surrendered to God (1 John 4:18). We should quit asking ourselves, "Am I of any use?" and accept the truth that we really are not of much use to Him. The issue is never of being of use, but of being of value to God Himself. Once we are totally surrendered to God, He will work through us all the time.

THE DISCIPLINE OF SPIRITUAL PERSEVERANCE

"Be still, and know that I am God . . ."
(PSALM 46:10).

Perseverance is more than endurance. It is endurance combined with absolute assurance and certainty that what we are looking for is going to happen. Perseverance means more than just hanging on, which may be only exposing our fear of letting go and falling. Perseverance is our supreme effort of refusing to believe that our hero is going to be conquered. Our greatest fear is not that we will be damned, but that somehow Jesus Christ will be defeated. Also, our fear is that the very things our Lord stood for—love, justice, forgiveness, and kindness among men—will not win out in the end and will represent an unattainable goal for us. Then there is the call to spiritual perseverance. A call not to hang on and do nothing, but to work deliberately, knowing with certainty that God will never be defeated.

If our hopes seem to be experiencing disappointment right now, it simply means that they are being purified. Every hope or dream of the human mind will be fulfilled if it is noble and of God. But one of the greatest stresses in life is the stress of waiting for God. He brings fulfillment, "because you have kept My command to persevere . . ." (Revelation 3:10).

Continue to persevere spiritually.

THE DETERMINATION TO SERVE

"The Son of Man did not come to be served, but to serve . . ."
(MATTHEW 20:28).

Jesus also said, "Yet I am among you as the One who serves" (Luke 22:27). Paul's idea of service was the same as our Lord's—". . . ourselves your bondservants for Jesus' sake" (2 Corinthians 4:5). We somehow have the idea that a person called to the ministry is called to be different and above other people. But according to Jesus Christ, he is called to be a "doormat" for others—called to be their spiritual leader, but never their superior. Paul said, "I know how to be abased . . ." (Philippians 4:12). Paul's idea of service was to pour his life out to the last drop for others. And whether he received praise or blame made no difference. As long as there was one human being who did not know Jesus, Paul felt a debt of service to that person until he did come to know Him. But the chief motivation behind Paul's service was not love for others but love for his Lord. If our devotion is to the cause of humanity, we will be quickly defeated and broken-hearted, since we will often be confronted with a great deal of ingratitude from other people. But if we are motivated by our love for God, no amount of ingratitude will be able to hinder us from serving one another.

Paul's understanding of how Christ had dealt with him is the secret behind his determination to serve others. "I was formerly a blasphemer, a persecutor, and an insolent man . . ." (1 Timothy 1:13). In other words, no matter how badly others may have treated Paul, they could never have treated him with the same degree of spite and hatred with which he had treated Jesus Christ. Once we realize that Jesus has served us even to the depths of our meagerness, our selfishness, and our sin, nothing we encounter from others will be able to exhaust our determination to serve others for His sake.

THE DELIGHT OF SACRIFICE

"I will very gladly spend and be spent for your souls . . ."
(2 CORINTHIANS 12:15).

Once "the love of God has been poured out in our hearts by the Holy Spirit," we deliberately begin to identify ourselves with Jesus Christ's interests and purposes in others' lives (Romans 5:5). And Jesus has an interest in every individual person. We have no right in Christian service to be guided by our own interests and desires. In fact, this is one of the greatest tests of our relationship with Jesus Christ. The delight of sacrifice is that I lay down my life for my Friend, Jesus (see John 15:13). I don't throw my life away, but I willingly and deliberately lay it down for Him and His interests in other people. And I do this for no cause or purpose of my own. Paul spent his life for only one purpose—that he might win people to Jesus Christ. Paul always attracted people to his Lord, but never to himself. He said, "I have become all things to all men, that I might by all means save some" (1 Corinthians 9:22).

When someone thinks that to develop a holy life he must always be alone with God, he is no longer of any use to others. This is like putting himself on a pedestal and isolating himself from the rest of society. Paul was a holy person, but wherever he went Jesus Christ was always allowed to help Himself to his life. Many of us are interested only in our own goals, and Jesus cannot help Himself to our lives. But if we are totally surrendered to Him, we have no goals of our own to serve. Paul said that he knew how to be a "doormat" without resenting it, because the motivation of his life was devotion to Jesus. We tend to be devoted, not to Jesus Christ, but to the things which allow us more spiritual freedom than total surrender to Him would allow. Freedom was not Paul's motive at all. In fact, he stated, "I could wish that I myself were accursed from Christ for my brethren . . ." (Romans 9:3). Had Paul lost his ability to reason? Not at all! For someone who is in love, this is not an overstatement. And Paul was in love with Jesus Christ.

THE DESTITUTION OF SERVICE

". . . though the more abundantly I love you, the less I am loved"
(2 CORINTHIANS 12:15).

Natural human love expects something in return. But Paul is saying, "It doesn't really matter to me whether you love me or not. I am willing to be completely destitute anyway; willing to be poverty-stricken, not just for your sakes, but also that I may be able to get you to God." "For you know the grace of our Lord Jesus Christ, that though He was rich, yet for your sakes He became poor . . ." (2 Corinthians 8:9). And Paul's idea of service was the same as our Lord's. He did not care how high the cost was to himself—he would gladly pay it. It was a joyful thing to Paul.

The institutional church's idea of a servant of God is not at all like Jesus Christ's idea. His idea is that we serve Him by being the servants of others. Jesus Christ actually "out-socialized" the socialists. He said that in His kingdom the greatest one would be the servant of all (see Matthew 23:11). The real test of a saint is not one's willingness to preach the gospel, but one's willingness to do something like washing the disciples' feet—that is, being willing to do those things that seem unimportant in human estimation but count as everything to God. It was Paul's delight to spend his life for God's interests in other people, and he did not care what it cost. But before we will serve, we stop to ponder our personal and financial concerns—"What if God wants me to go over there? And what about my salary? What is the climate like there? Who will take care of me? A person must consider all these things." All that is an indication that we have reservations about serving God. But the apostle Paul had no conditions or reservations. Paul focused his life on Jesus Christ's idea of a New Testament saint; that is, not one who merely proclaims the gospel, but one who becomes broken bread and poured-out wine in the hands of Jesus Christ for the sake of others.

"IF YOU HAD KNOWN!"

"If you had known . . . in this your day, the things that make for your peace! But now they are hidden from your eyes"
(LUKE 19:42).

Jesus entered Jerusalem triumphantly and the city was stirred to its very foundations, but a strange god was there—the pride of the Pharisees. It was a god that seemed religious and upright, but Jesus compared it to "whitewashed tombs which indeed appear beautiful outwardly, but inside are full of dead men's bones and all uncleanness" (Matthew 23:27).

What is it that blinds you to the peace of God "in this *your* day"? Do you have a strange god—not a disgusting monster but perhaps an unholy nature that controls your life? More than once God has brought me face to face with a strange god in my life, and I knew that I should have given it up, but I didn't do it. I got through the crisis "by the skin of my teeth," only to find myself still under the control of that strange god. I am blind to the very things that make for my own peace. It is a shocking thing that we can be in the exact place where the Spirit of God should be having His completely unhindered way with us, and yet we only make matters worse, increasing our blame in God's eyes.

"If you had known . . . ." God's words here cut directly to the heart, with the tears of Jesus behind them. These words imply responsibility for our own faults. God holds us accountable for what we refuse to see or are unable to see because of our sin. And "now they are hidden from your eyes" because you have never completely yielded your nature to Him. Oh, the deep, unending sadness for what might have been! God never again opens the doors that have been closed. He opens other doors, but He reminds us that there are doors which we have shut—doors which had no need to be shut. Never be afraid when God brings back your past. Let your memory have its way with you. It is a minister of God bringing its rebuke and sorrow to you. God will turn what might have been into a wonderful lesson of growth for the future.

THE WAY TO PERMANENT FAITH

"Indeed the hour is coming . . . that you will be scattered . . ."
(JOHN 16:32).

Jesus was not rebuking the disciples in this passage. Their faith was real, but it was disordered and unfocused, and was not at work in the important realities of life. The disciples were scattered to their own concerns and they had interests apart from Jesus Christ. After we have the perfect relationship with God, through the sanctifying work of the Holy Spirit, our faith must be exercised in the realities of everyday life. We will be scattered, not into service but into the emptiness of our lives where we will see ruin and barrenness, to know what internal death to God's blessings means. Are we prepared for this? It is certainly not of our own choosing, but God engineers our circumstances to take us there. Until we have been through that experience, our faith is sustained only by feelings and by blessings. But once we get there, no matter where God may place us or what inner emptiness we experience, we can praise God that all is well. That is what is meant by faith being exercised in the realities of life.

". . . you . . . will leave Me alone." Have we been scattered and have we left Jesus alone by not seeing His providential care for us? Do we not see God at work in our circumstances? Dark times are allowed and come to us through the sovereignty of God. Are we prepared to let God do what He wants with us? Are we prepared to be separated from the outward, evident blessings of God? Until Jesus Christ is truly our Lord, we each have goals of our own which we serve. Our faith is real, but it is not yet permanent. And God is never in a hurry. If we are willing to wait, we will see God pointing out that we have been interested only in His blessings, instead of in God Himself. The sense of God's blessings is fundamental.

". . . be of good cheer, I have overcome the world" (16:33). Unyielding spiritual fortitude is what we need.

HIS AGONY AND OUR ACCESS

"Jesus came with them to a place called Gethsemane, and said to the disciples . . . . 'Stay here and watch with Me' "
(MATTHEW 26:36, 38).

We can never fully comprehend Christ's agony in the Garden of Gethsemane, but at least we don't have to misunderstand it. It is the agony of God and man in one Person, coming face to face with sin. We cannot learn about Gethsemane through personal experience. Gethsemane and Calvary represent something totally unique—they are the gateway into life for us.

It was not death on the cross that Jesus agonized over in Gethsemane. In fact, He stated very emphatically that He came with the purpose of dying. His concern here was that He might not get through this struggle as the Son of Man. He was confident of getting through it as the Son of God—Satan could not touch Him there. But Satan's assault was that our Lord would come through for us on His own solely as the Son of Man. If Jesus had done that, He could not have been our Savior (see Hebrews 9:11-15). Read the record of His agony in Gethsemane in light of His earlier wilderness temptation—". . . the devil . . . departed from Him until an opportune time" (Luke 4:13). In Gethsemane, Satan came back and was overthrown again. Satan's final assault against our Lord as the *Son of Man* was in Gethsemane.

The agony in Gethsemane was the agony of the Son of God in fulfilling His destiny as the Savior of the world. The veil is pulled back here to reveal all that it cost Him to make it possible for us to become sons of God. His agony was the basis for the simplicity of our salvation. The Cross of Christ was a triumph for the *Son of Man*. It was not only a sign that our Lord had triumphed, but that He had triumphed to save the human race. Because of what the Son of Man went through, every human being has been provided with a way of access into the very presence of God.

THE COLLISION OF GOD AND SIN

". . . who Himself bore our sins in His own body on the tree . . ."
(1 PETER 2:24).

The Cross of Christ is the revealed truth of God's judgment on sin. Never associate the idea of martyrdom with the Cross of Christ. It was the supreme triumph, and it shook the very foundations of hell. There is nothing in time or eternity more absolutely certain and irrefutable than what Jesus Christ accomplished on the Cross—He made it possible for the entire human race to be brought back into a right-standing relationship with God. He made redemption the foundation of human life; that is, He made a way for every person to have fellowship with God.

The Cross was not something that *happened* to Jesus—He came to die; the Cross was His purpose in coming. He is "the Lamb slain from the foundation of the world" (Revelation 13:8). The incarnation of Christ would have no meaning without the Cross. Beware of separating *"God was manifested in the flesh . . ."* from *". . . He made Him . . . to be sin for us . . ."* (1 Timothy 3:16; 2 Corinthians 5:21). The purpose of the incarnation was redemption. God came in the flesh to take sin away, not to accomplish something for Himself. The Cross is the central event in time and eternity, and the answer to all the problems of both.

The Cross is not the cross of a man, but the Cross of God, and it can never be fully comprehended through human experience. The Cross is God exhibiting His nature. It is the gate through which any and every individual can enter into oneness with God. But it is not a gate we pass right through; it is one where we abide in the life that is found there.

The heart of salvation is the Cross of Christ. The reason salvation is so easy to obtain is that it cost God so much. The Cross was the place where God and sinful man merged with a tremendous collision and where the way to life was opened. But all the cost and pain of the collision was absorbed by the heart of God.

WHY WE LACK UNDERSTANDING

"He commanded them that they should tell no one the things they had seen, till the Son of Man had risen from the dead"
(MARK 9:9).

As the disciples were commanded, you should also say nothing until the Son of Man has risen in you—until the life of the risen Christ so dominates you that you truly understand what He taught while here on earth. When you grow and develop the right condition inwardly, the words Jesus spoke become so clear that you are amazed you did not grasp them before. In fact, you were not able to understand them before because you had not yet developed the proper spiritual condition to deal with them.

Our Lord doesn't hide these things from us, but we are not prepared to receive them until we are in the right condition in our spiritual life. Jesus said, "I still have many things to say to you, but you cannot bear them now" (John 16:12). We must have a oneness with His risen life before we are prepared to bear any particular truth from Him. Do we really know anything about the indwelling of the risen life of Jesus? The evidence that we do is that His Word is becoming understandable to us. God cannot reveal anything to us if we don't have His Spirit. And our own unyielding and headstrong opinions will effectively prevent God from revealing anything to us. But our insensible thinking will end immediately once His resurrection life has its way with us.

". . . tell no one . . . ." But so many people do tell what they saw on the Mount of Transfiguration—their mountaintop experience. They have seen a vision and they testify to it, but there is no connection between what they say and how they live. Their lives don't add up because the Son of Man has not yet risen in them. How long will it be before His resurrection life is formed and evident in you and in me?

HIS RESURRECTION DESTINY

**"Ought not the Christ to have suffered these things
and to enter into His glory?"**
(LUKE 24:26).

O ur Lord's Cross is the gateway into His life. His resurrection means that He has the power to convey His life to me. When I was born again, I received the very life of the risen Lord from Jesus Himself.

Christ's resurrection destiny—His foreordained purpose—was to bring "many sons to glory" (Hebrews 2:10). The fulfilling of His destiny gives Him the right to make us sons and daughters of God. We never have exactly the same relationship to God that the Son of God has, but we are brought by the Son into the relation of sonship. When our Lord rose from the dead, He rose to an absolutely new life—a life He had never lived before He was God Incarnate. He rose to a life that had never been before. And what His resurrection means for us is that we are raised to His risen life, not to our old life. One day we will have a body like His glorious body, but we can know here and now the power and effectiveness of His resurrection and can "walk in newness of life" (Romans 6:4). Paul's determined purpose was to "know Him *and the power of His resurrection*" (Philippians 3:10).

Jesus prayed, ". . . as You have given Him authority over all flesh that He should give eternal life to as many as You have given Him" (John 17:2). The term *Holy Spirit* is actually another name for the experience of eternal life working in human beings here and now. The Holy Spirit is the deity of God who continues to apply the power of the atonement by the Cross of Christ to our lives. Thank God for the glorious and majestic truth that His Spirit can work the very nature of Jesus into us, if we will only obey Him.

HAVE YOU SEEN JESUS?

"After that, He appeared in another form to two of them . . ."
(MARK 16:12).

Being saved and seeing Jesus are not the same thing. Many people who have never seen Jesus have received and share in God's grace. But once you have seen Him, you can never be the same. Other things will not have the appeal they did before.

You should always recognize the difference between what you see Jesus to be and what He has done for you. If you see only what He has done for you, your God is not big enough. But if you have had a vision, seeing Jesus as He really is, experiences can come and go, yet you will endure "as seeing Him who is invisible" (Hebrews 11:27). The man who was blind from birth did not know who Jesus was until Christ appeared and revealed Himself to him (see John 9). Jesus appears to those for whom He has done something, but we cannot order or predict when He will come. He may appear suddenly, at any turn. Then you can exclaim, "Now I see Him!" (see John 9:25).

Jesus must appear to you and to your friend individually; no one can see Jesus with your eyes. And division takes place when one has seen Him and the other has not. You cannot bring your friend to the point of seeing; God must do it. Have you seen Jesus? If so, you will want others to see Him too. "And they went and told it to the rest, but they did not believe them either" (Mark 16:13). When you see Him, you must tell, even if they don't believe.

O could I tell, you surely would believe it!
    O could I only say what I have seen!
How should I tell or how can you receive it,
    How, till He bringeth you where I have been?

COMPLETE AND EFFECTIVE DECISION ABOUT SIN

". . . our old man was crucified with Him, that the body of sin might be done away with, that we should no longer be slaves of sin"
(ROMANS 6:6).

CO-CRUCIFIXION. Have you made the following decision about sin—that it must be completely killed in you? It takes a long time to come to the point of making this complete and effective decision about sin. It is, however, the greatest moment in your life once you decide that sin must die in you—not simply be restrained, suppressed, or counteracted, but crucified—just as Jesus Christ died for the sin of the world. No one can bring anyone else to this decision. We may be mentally and spiritually convinced, but what we need to do is actually make the decision that Paul urged us to do in this passage.

Pull yourself up, take some time alone with God, and make this important decision, saying, "Lord, identify me with Your death until I know that sin is dead in me." Make the moral decision that sin in you must be put to death.

This was not some divine future expectation on the part of Paul, but was a very radical and definite experience in his life. Are you prepared to let the Spirit of God search you until you know what the level and nature of sin is in your life—to see the very things that struggle against God's Spirit in you? If so, will you then agree with God's verdict on the nature of sin—that it should be identified with the death of Jesus? You cannot "reckon yourselves to be dead indeed to sin" (6:11) unless you have radically dealt with the issue of your will before God.

Have you entered into the glorious privilege of being crucified with Christ, until all that remains in your flesh and blood is His life? "I have been crucified with Christ; it is no longer I who live, but Christ lives in me . . ." (Galatians 2:20).

COMPLETE AND EFFECTIVE DIVINITY

"If we have been united together in the likeness of His death, certainly we also shall be in the likeness of His resurrection . . ."
(ROMANS 6:5).

CO-RESURRECTION. The proof that I have experienced crucifixion with Jesus is that I have a definite likeness to Him. The Spirit of Jesus entering me rearranges my personal life before God. The resurrection of Jesus has given Him the authority to give the life of God to me, and the experiences of my life must now be built on the foundation of His life. I can have the resurrection life of Jesus here and now, and it will exhibit itself through holiness.

The idea all through the apostle Paul's writings is that after the decision to be identified with Jesus in His death has been made, the resurrection life of Jesus penetrates every bit of my human nature. It takes the omnipotence of God—His complete and effective divinity—to live the life of the Son of God in human flesh. The Holy Spirit cannot be accepted as a guest in merely one room of the house—He invades all of it. And once I decide that my "old man" (that is, my heredity of sin) should be identified with the death of Jesus, the Holy Spirit invades me. He takes charge of everything. My part is to walk in the light and to obey all that He reveals to me. Once I have made that important decision about sin, it is easy to "reckon" that I am actually "dead indeed to sin," because I find the life of Jesus in me all the time (Romans 6:11). Just as there is only one kind of humanity, there is only one kind of holiness—the holiness of Jesus. And it is His holiness that has been given to me. God puts the holiness of His Son into me, and I belong to a new spiritual order.

COMPLETE AND EFFECTIVE DOMINION

"Death no longer has dominion over Him. . . . the life that
He lives, He lives to God. Likewise you also, reckon yourselves to
be dead indeed to sin, but alive to God . . ."
(ROMANS 6:9–11).

CO-ETERNAL LIFE. Eternal life is the life which Jesus Christ exhibited on the human level. And it is this same life, not simply a copy of it, which is made evident in our mortal flesh when we are born again. Eternal life is not a gift from God; eternal life is the gift *of God.* The energy and the power which was so very evident in Jesus will be exhibited in us by an act of the absolute sovereign grace of God, once we have made that complete and effective decision about sin.

"You shall receive power when the Holy Spirit has come upon you . . ." (Acts 1:8)—not power as a gift from the Holy Spirit; the power *is* the Holy Spirit, not something that He gives us. The life that was in Jesus becomes ours because of His Cross, once we make the decision to be identified with Him. If it is difficult to get right with God, it is because we refuse to make this moral decision about sin. But once we do decide, the full life of God comes in immediately. Jesus came to give us an endless supply of life— ". . . that you may be filled with all the fullness of God" (Ephesians 3:19). Eternal life has nothing to do with time. It is the life which Jesus lived when He was down here, and the only Source of life is the Lord Jesus Christ.

Even the weakest saint can experience the power of the deity of the Son of God, when he is willing to "let go." But any effort to "hang on" to the least bit of our own power will only diminish the life of Jesus in us. We have to keep letting go, and slowly, but surely, the great full life of God will invade us, penetrating every part. Then Jesus will have complete and effective dominion in us, and people will take notice that we have been with Him.

WHAT TO DO WHEN YOUR BURDEN IS OVERWHELMING

"Cast your burden on the Lord . . ."
(PSALM 55:22).

We must recognize the difference between burdens that are right for us to bear and burdens that are wrong. We should never bear the burdens of sin or doubt, but there are some burdens placed on us by God which He does not intend to lift off. God wants us to roll them back on Him—to literally "cast your burden," which He has given you, "on the Lord . . . ." If we set out to serve God and do His work but get out of touch with Him, the sense of responsibility we feel will be overwhelming and defeating. But if we will only roll back on God the burdens He has placed on us, He will take away that immense feeling of responsibility, replacing it with an awareness and understanding of Himself and His presence.

Many servants set out to serve God with great courage and with the right motives. But with no intimate fellowship with Jesus Christ, they are soon defeated. They do not know what to do with their burden, and it produces weariness in their lives. Others will see this and say, "What a sad end to something that had such a great beginning!"

"Cast your burden on the Lord . . . ." You have been bearing it all, but you need to deliberately place one end on God's shoulder. ". . . the government will be upon His shoulder" (Isaiah 9:6). Commit to God whatever burden He has placed on you. Don't just cast it aside, but put it over onto Him and place yourself there with it. You will see that your burden is then lightened by the sense of companionship. But you should never try to separate yourself from your burden.

INNER INVINCIBILITY

"Take My yoke upon you and learn from Me . . ."
(MATTHEW 11:29).

Whom the Lord loves He chastens . . ." (Hebrews 12:6). How petty our complaining is! Our Lord begins to bring us to the point where we can have fellowship with Him, only to hear us moan and groan, saying, "Oh Lord, just let me be like other people!" Jesus is asking us to get beside Him and take one end of the yoke, so that we can pull together. That's why Jesus says to us, "My yoke is easy and My burden is light" (Matthew 11:30). Are you closely identified with the Lord Jesus like that? If so, you will thank God when you feel the pressure of His hand upon you.

". . . to those who have no might He increases strength" (Isaiah 40:29). God comes and takes us out of our emotionalism, and then our complaining turns into a hymn of praise. The only way to know the strength of God is to take the yoke of Jesus upon us and to learn from Him.

". . . the joy of the Lord is your strength" (Nehemiah 8:10). Where do the saints get their joy? If we did not know some Christians well, we might think from just observing them that they have no burdens at all to bear. But we must lift the veil from our eyes. The fact that the peace, light, and joy of God is in them is proof that a burden is there as well. The burden that God places on us squeezes the grapes in our lives and produces the wine, but most of us see only the wine and not the burden. No power on earth or in hell can conquer the Spirit of God living within the human spirit; it creates an inner invincibility.

If your life is producing only a whine, instead of the wine, then ruthlessly kick it out. It is definitely a crime for a Christian to be weak in God's strength.

AM I BLESSED LIKE THIS?

"Blessed are . . ."
(MATTHEW 5:3–11).

When we first read the statements of Jesus, they seem wonderfully simple and unstartling, and they sink unnoticed into our subconscious minds. For instance, the Beatitudes initially seem to be merely soothing and beautiful precepts for overly spiritual and seemingly useless people, but of very little practical use in the rigid, fast-paced workdays of the world in which we live. We soon find, however, that the Beatitudes contain the "dynamite" of the Holy Spirit. And they "explode" when the circumstances of our lives cause them to do so. When the Holy Spirit brings to our remembrance one of the Beatitudes, we say, "What a startling statement that is!" Then we must decide whether or not we will accept the tremendous spiritual upheaval that will be produced in our circumstances if we obey His words. That is the way the Spirit of God works. We do not need to be born again to apply the Sermon on the Mount literally. The literal interpretation of the Sermon on the Mount is as easy as child's play. But the interpretation by the Spirit of God as He applies our Lord's statements to our circumstances is the strict and difficult work of a saint.

The teachings of Jesus are all out of proportion when compared to our natural way of looking at things, and they come to us initially with astonishing discomfort. We gradually have to conform our walk and conversation to the precepts of Jesus Christ as the Holy Spirit applies them to our circumstances. The Sermon on the Mount is not a set of rules and regulations—it is a picture of the life we will live when the Holy Spirit is having His unhindered way with us.

THE WAY TO PURITY

"Those things which proceed out of the mouth come from
the heart . . . . For out of the heart proceed evil thoughts, murders,
adulteries, fornications, thefts, false witness, blasphemies.
These are the things which defile a man . . ."
(MATTHEW 15:18–20).

Initially we trust in our ignorance, calling it innocence, and next we trust our innocence, calling it purity. Then when we hear these strong statements from our Lord, we shrink back, saying, "But I never felt any of those awful things in my heart." We resent what He reveals. Either Jesus Christ is the supreme authority on the human heart, or He is not worth paying any attention to. Am I prepared to trust the penetration of His Word into my heart, or would I prefer to trust my own "innocent ignorance"? If I will take an honest look at myself, becoming fully aware of my so-called innocence and putting it to the test, I am very likely to have a rude awakening that what Jesus Christ said is true, and I will be appalled at the possibilities of the evil and the wrong within me. But as long as I remain under the false security of my own "innocence," I am living in a fool's paradise. If I have never been an openly rude and abusive person, the only reason is my own cowardice coupled with the sense of protection I receive from living a civilized life. But when I am open and completely exposed before God, I find that Jesus Christ is right in His diagnosis of me.

The only thing that truly provides protection is the redemption of Jesus Christ. If I will simply hand myself over to Him, I will never have to experience the terrible possibilities that lie within my heart. Purity is something far too deep for me to arrive at naturally. But when the Holy Spirit comes into me, He brings into the center of my personal life the very Spirit that was exhibited in the life of Jesus Christ, namely, the *Holy* Spirit, which is absolute unblemished purity.

THE WAY TO KNOWLEDGE

"If anyone wills to do His will, he shall know concerning the doctrine . . ." (JOHN 7:17).

The golden rule to follow to obtain spiritual understanding is not one of intellectual pursuit, but one of obedience. If a person wants scientific knowledge, then intellectual curiosity must be his guide. But if he desires knowledge and insight into the teachings of Jesus Christ, he can only obtain it through obedience. If spiritual things seem dark and hidden to me, then I can be sure that there is a point of disobedience somewhere in my life. Intellectual darkness is the result of ignorance, but spiritual darkness is the result of something that I do not intend to obey.

No one ever receives a word from God without instantly being put to the test regarding it. We disobey and then wonder why we are not growing spiritually. Jesus said, "If you bring your gift to the altar, and there remember that your brother has something against you, leave your gift there before the altar, and go your way. First be reconciled to your brother, and then come and offer your gift" (Matthew 5:23–24). He is saying, in essence, "Don't say another word to me; first be obedient by making things right." The teachings of Jesus hit us where we live. We cannot stand as impostors before Him for even one second. He instructs us down to the very last detail. The Spirit of God uncovers our spirit of self-vindication and makes us sensitive to things that we have never even thought of before.

When Jesus drives something home to you through His Word, don't try to evade it. If you do, you will become a religious impostor. Examine the things you tend simply to shrug your shoulders about, and where you have refused to be obedient, and you will know why you are not growing spiritually. As Jesus said, "*First . . . go . . . .*" Even at the risk of being thought of as fanatical, you must obey what God tells you.

GOD'S PURPOSE OR MINE?

"He made His disciples get into the boat and go before Him to the other side . . ." (MARK 6:45).

We tend to think that if Jesus Christ compels us to do something and we are obedient to Him, He will lead us to great success. We should never have the thought that our dreams of success are God's purpose for us. In fact, His purpose may be exactly the opposite. We have the idea that God is leading us toward a particular end or a desired goal, but He is not. The question of whether or not we arrive at a particular goal is of little importance, and reaching it becomes merely an episode along the way. What we see as only the process of reaching a particular end, God sees as the goal itself.

What is my vision of God's purpose for me? Whatever it may be, His purpose is for me to depend on Him and on His power *now*. If I can stay calm, faithful, and unconfused while in the middle of the turmoil of life, the goal of the purpose of God is being accomplished in me. God is not working toward a particular finish—His purpose is the process itself. What He desires for me is that I see "Him walking on the sea" with no shore, no success, nor goal in sight, but simply having the absolute certainty that everything is all right because I see "Him walking on the sea" (6:49). It is the process, not the outcome, that is glorifying to God.

God's training is for now, not later. His purpose is for this very minute, not for sometime in the future. We have nothing to do with what will follow our obedience, and we are wrong to concern ourselves with it. What people call preparation, God sees as the goal itself.

God's purpose is to enable me to see that He can walk on the storms of my life right now. If we have a further goal in mind, we are not paying enough attention to the present time. However, if we realize that moment-by-moment obedience is the goal, then each moment as it comes is precious.

DO YOU SEE JESUS IN YOUR CLOUDS?

"Behold, He is coming with clouds . . ." (REVELATION 1:7).

In the Bible clouds are always associated with God. Clouds are the sorrows, sufferings, or providential circumstances, within or without our personal lives, which actually seem to contradict the sovereignty of God. Yet it is through these very clouds that the Spirit of God is teaching us how to walk by faith. If there were never any clouds in our lives, we would have no faith. "The clouds are the dust of His feet" (Nahum 1:3). They are a sign that God is there. What a revelation it is to know that sorrow, bereavement, and suffering are actually the clouds that come along with God! God cannot come near us without clouds—He does not come in clear-shining brightness.

It is not true to say that God wants to teach us something in our trials. Through every cloud He brings our way, He wants us to *unlearn* something. His purpose in using the cloud is to simplify our beliefs until our relationship with Him is exactly like that of a child—a relationship simply between God and our own souls, and where other people are but shadows. Until other people become shadows to us, clouds and darkness will be ours every once in a while. Is our relationship with God becoming more simple than it has ever been?

There is a connection between the strange providential circumstances allowed by God and what we know of Him, and we have to learn to interpret the mysteries of life in the light of our knowledge of God. Until we can come face to face with the deepest, darkest fact of life without damaging our view of God's character, we do not yet know Him.

". . . they were fearful as they entered the cloud" (Luke 9:34). Is there anyone except Jesus in your cloud? If so, it will only get darker until you get to the place where there is "no one anymore, but only Jesus . . ." (Mark 9:8; also see verses 2–7).

THE TEACHING OF DISILLUSIONMENT

"Jesus did not commit Himself to them . . . , for He knew what was in man" (JOHN 2:24–25).

Disillusionment means having no more misconceptions, false impressions, and false judgments in life; it means being free from these deceptions. However, though no longer deceived, our experience of disillusionment may actually leave us cynical and overly critical in our judgment of others. But the disillusionment that comes from God brings us to the point where we see people as they really are, yet without any cynicism or any stinging and bitter criticism. Many of the things in life that inflict the greatest injury, grief, or pain, stem from the fact that we suffer from illusions. We are not true to one another as *facts*, seeing each other as we really are; we are only true to our misconceived *ideas* of one another. According to our thinking, everything is either delightful and good, or it is evil, malicious, and cowardly.

Refusing to be disillusioned is the cause of much of the suffering of human life. And this is how that suffering happens—if we love someone, but do not love God, we demand total perfection and righteousness from that person, and when we do not get it we become cruel and vindictive; yet we are demanding of a human being something which he or she cannot possibly give. There is only one Being who can completely satisfy to the absolute depth of the hurting human heart, and that is the Lord Jesus Christ. Our Lord is so obviously uncompromising with regard to every human relationship because He knows that every relationship that is not based on faithfulness to Himself will end in disaster. Our Lord trusted no one, and never placed His faith in people, yet He was never suspicious or bitter. Our Lord's confidence in God, and in what God's grace could do for anyone, was so perfect that He never despaired, never giving up hope for any person. If our trust is placed in human beings, we will end up despairing of everyone.

BECOMING ENTIRELY HIS

"Let patience have its perfect work, that you may be perfect and complete, lacking nothing" (JAMES 1:4).

Many of us appear to be all right in general, but there are still some areas in which we are careless and lazy; it is not a matter of sin, but the remnants of our carnal life that tend to make us careless. Carelessness is an insult to the Holy Spirit. We should have no carelessness about us either in the way we worship God, or even in the way we eat and drink.

Not only must our relationship to God be right, but the outward expression of that relationship must also be right. Ultimately, God will allow nothing to escape; every detail of our lives is under His scrutiny. God will bring us back in countless ways to the same point over and over again. And He never tires of bringing us back to that one point until we learn the lesson, because His purpose is to produce the finished product. It may be a problem arising from our impulsive nature, but again and again, with the most persistent patience, God has brought us back to that one particular point. Or the problem may be our idle and wandering thinking, or our independent nature and self-interest. Through this process, God is trying to impress upon us the one thing that is not entirely right in our lives.

We have been having a wonderful time in our studies over the revealed truth of God's redemption, and our hearts are perfect toward Him. And His wonderful work in us makes us know that overall we are right with Him. "Let patience have its perfect work . . . ." The Holy Spirit speaking through James said, "Now let your patience become a finished product." Beware of becoming careless over the small details of life and saying, "Oh, that will have to do for now." Whatever it may be, God will point it out with persistence until we become entirely His.

LEARNING ABOUT HIS WAYS

**"When Jesus finished commanding His twelve disciples . . .
He departed from there to teach and to preach in their cities"**
(MATTHEW 11:1).

He comes where He commands us to leave. If you stayed home when God told you to go because you were so concerned about your own people there, then you actually robbed them of the teaching of Jesus Christ Himself. When you obeyed and left all the consequences to God, the Lord went into your city to teach, but as long as you were disobedient, you blocked His way. Watch where you begin to debate with Him and put what you call your duty into competition with His commands. If you say, "I know that He told me to go, but my duty is here," it simply means that you do not believe that Jesus means what He says.

He teaches where He instructs us not to teach.

"Master . . . let us make three tabernacles . . ." (Luke 9:33).

Are we playing the part of an amateur providence, trying to play God's role in the lives of others? Are we so noisy in our instruction of other people that God cannot get near them? We must learn to keep our mouths shut and our spirits alert. God wants to instruct us regarding His Son, and He wants to turn our times of prayer into mounts of transfiguration. When we become certain that God is going to work in a particular way, He will never work in that way again.

He works where He sends us to wait.

". . . tarry . . . until . . ." (Luke 24:49).

"Wait on the Lord" and He will work (Psalm 37:34). But don't wait sulking spiritually and feeling sorry for yourself, just because you can't see one inch in front of you! Are we detached enough from our own spiritual fits of emotion to "wait patiently for Him"? (37:7). Waiting is not sitting with folded hands doing nothing, but it is learning to do what we are told.

These are some of the facets of His ways that we rarely recognize.

THE TEACHING OF ADVERSITY

**"In the world you will have tribulation; but be of good cheer,
I have overcome the world"** (JOHN 16:33).

The typical view of the Christian life is that it means being delivered from all adversity. But it actually means being delivered *in* adversity, which is something very different. "He who dwells in the secret place of the Most High shall abide under the shadow of the Almighty. No evil shall befall you, nor shall any plague come near your dwelling . . ." (Psalm 91:1, 10)—the place where you are at one with God.

If you are a child of God, you will certainly encounter adversities, but Jesus says you should not be surprised when they come. "In the world you will have tribulation; but be of good cheer, I have overcome the world." He is saying, "There is nothing for you to fear." The same people who refused to talk about their adversities before they were saved often complain and worry after being born again because they have the wrong idea of what it means to live the life of a saint.

God does not give us overcoming life—He gives us life as we overcome. The strain of life is what builds our strength. If there is no strain, there will be no strength. Are you asking God to give you life, liberty, and joy? He cannot, unless you are willing to accept the strain. And once you face the strain, you will immediately get the strength. Overcome your own timidity and take the first step. Then God will give you nourishment—"To him who overcomes I will give to eat from the tree of life . . ." (Revelation 2:7). If you completely give of yourself physically, you become exhausted. But when you give of yourself spiritually, you get more strength. God never gives us strength for tomorrow, or for the next hour, but only for the strain of the moment. Our temptation is to face adversities from the standpoint of our own common sense. But a saint can "be of good cheer" even when seemingly defeated by adversities, because victory is absurdly impossible to everyone, except God.

THE COMPELLING PURPOSE OF GOD

"He ... said to them, 'Behold, we are going up to Jerusalem ...' " (LUKE 18:31).

Jerusalem, in the life of our Lord, represents the place where He reached the culmination of His Father's will. Jesus said, "I do not seek My own will but the will of the Father who sent Me" (John 5:30). Seeking to do "the will of the Father" was the one dominating concern throughout our Lord's life. And whatever He encountered along the way, whether joy or sorrow, success or failure, He was never deterred from that purpose. "... He steadfastly set His face to go to Jerusalem ..." (Luke 9:51).

The greatest thing for us to remember is that we go up to Jerusalem to fulfill God's purpose, not our own. In the natural life our ambitions are our own, but in the Christian life we have no goals of our own. We talk so much today about our decisions for Christ, our determination to be Christians, and our decisions for this and that, but in the New Testament the only aspect that is brought out is the compelling purpose of God. "You did not choose Me, but I chose you ..." (John 15:16).

We are not taken into a conscious agreement with God's purpose—we are taken into God's purpose with no awareness of it at all. We have no idea what God's goal may be; as we continue, His purpose becomes even more and more vague. God's aim appears to have missed the mark, because we are too nearsighted to see the target at which He is aiming. At the beginning of the Christian life, we have our own ideas as to what God's purpose is. We say, "God means for me to go over there," and, "God has called me to do this special work." We do what we think is right, and yet the compelling purpose of God remains upon us. The work we do is of no account when compared with the compelling purpose of God. It is simply the scaffolding surrounding His work and His plan. "He took the twelve aside ..." (Luke 18:31). God takes us aside all the time. We have not yet understood all there is to know of the compelling purpose of God.

THE BRAVE FRIENDSHIP OF GOD

"He took the twelve aside . . ." (LUKE 18:31).

Oh, the bravery of God in trusting us! Do you say, "But He has been unwise to choose me, because there is nothing good in me and I have no value"? That is exactly why He chose you. As long as you think that you are of value to Him He cannot choose you, because you have purposes of your own to serve. But if you will allow Him to take you to the end of your own self-sufficiency, then He can choose you to go with Him "to Jerusalem" (18:31). And that will mean the fulfillment of purposes which He does not discuss with you.

We tend to say that because a person has natural ability, he will make a good Christian. It is not a matter of our equipment, but a matter of our poverty; not of what we bring with us, but of what God puts into us; not a matter of natural virtues, of strength of character, of knowledge, or of experience—all of that is of no avail in this concern. The only thing of value is being taken into the compelling purpose of God and being made His friends (see 1 Corinthians 1:26–31). God's friendship is with people who know their poverty. He can accomplish nothing with the person who thinks that he is of use to God. As Christians we are not here for our own purpose at all—we are here for the purpose of God, and the two are not the same. We do not know what God's compelling purpose is, but whatever happens, we must maintain our relationship with Him. We must never allow anything to damage our relationship with God, but if something does damage it, we must take the time to make it right again. The most important aspect of Christianity is not the work we do, but the relationship we maintain and the surrounding influence and qualities produced by that relationship. That is all God asks us to give our attention to, and it is the one thing that is continually under attack.

THE BEWILDERING CALL OF GOD

" '. . . and all things that are written by the prophets concerning the Son of Man will be accomplished.' . . . But they understood none of these things . . ." (LUKE 18:31, 34).

God called Jesus Christ to what seemed absolute disaster. And Jesus Christ called His disciples to see Him put to death, leading every one of them to the place where their hearts were broken. His life was an absolute failure from every standpoint except God's. But what seemed to be failure from man's standpoint was a triumph from God's standpoint, because God's purpose is never the same as man's purpose.

This bewildering call of God comes into our lives as well. The call of God can never be understood absolutely or explained externally; it is a call that can only be perceived and understood internally by our true inner nature. The call of God is like the call of the sea—no one hears it except the person who has the nature of the sea in him. What God calls us to cannot be definitely stated, because His call is simply to be His friend to accomplish His own purposes. Our real test is in truly believing that God knows what He desires. The things that happen do not happen by chance—they happen entirely by the decree of God. God is sovereignly working out His own purposes.

If we are in fellowship and oneness with God and recognize that He is taking us into His purposes, then we will no longer strive to find out what His purposes are. As we grow in the Christian life, it becomes simpler to us, because we are less inclined to say, "I wonder why God allowed this or that?" And we begin to see that the compelling purpose of God lies behind everything in life, and that God is divinely shaping us into oneness with that purpose. A Christian is someone who trusts in the knowledge and the wisdom of God, not in his own abilities. If we have a purpose of our own, it destroys the simplicity and the calm, relaxed pace which should be characteristic of the children of God.

THE CROSS IN PRAYER

"In that day you will ask in My name . . ." (JOHN 16:26).

We too often think of the Cross of Christ as something we have to get through, yet we get *through* for the purpose of getting *into* it. The Cross represents only one thing for us—complete, entire, absolute identification with the Lord Jesus Christ—and there is nothing in which this identification is more real to us than in prayer.

"Your Father knows the things you have need of before you ask Him" (Matthew 6:8). Then why should we ask? The point of prayer is not to get answers from God, but to have perfect and complete oneness with Him. If we pray only because we want answers, we will become irritated and angry with God. We receive an answer every time we pray, but it does not always come in the way we expect, and our spiritual irritation shows our refusal to identify ourselves truly with our Lord in prayer. We are not here to prove that God answers prayer, but to be living trophies of God's grace.

". . . I do not say to you that I shall pray the Father for you; for the Father Himself loves you . . ." (John 16:26–27). Have you reached such a level of intimacy with God that the only thing that can account for your prayer life is that it has become one with the prayer life of Jesus Christ? Has our Lord exchanged your life with His vital life? If so, then "in that day" you will be so closely identified with Jesus that there will be no distinction.

When prayer seems to be unanswered, beware of trying to place the blame on someone else. That is always a trap of Satan. When you seem to have no answer, there is always a reason—God uses these times to give you deep personal instruction, and it is not for anyone else but you.

PRAYER IN THE FATHER'S HOUSE

"...they found Him in the temple....And He said to them,
'...Did you not know that I must be about My Father's business?'"
(LUKE 2:46, 49).

Our Lord's childhood was not immaturity waiting to grow into manhood—His childhood is an eternal fact. Am I a holy, innocent child of God as a result of my identification with my Lord and Savior? Do I look at my life as being in my Father's house? Is the Son of God living in His Father's house within me?

The only abiding reality is God Himself, and His order comes to me moment by moment. Am I continually in touch with the reality of God, or do I pray only when things have gone wrong—when there is some disturbance in my life? I must learn to identify myself closely with my Lord in ways of holy fellowship and oneness that some of us have not yet even begun to learn. "... I must be about My Father's business"—and I must learn to live every moment of my life in my Father's house.

Think about your own circumstances. Are you so closely identified with the Lord's life that you are simply a child of God, continually talking to Him and realizing that everything comes from His hands? Is the eternal Child in you living in His Father's house? Is the grace of His ministering life being worked out through you in your home, your business, and in your circle of friends? Have you been wondering why you are going through certain circumstances? In fact, it is not that *you* have to go through them. It is because of your relationship with the Son of God who comes, through the providential will of His Father, into your life. You must allow *Him* to have His way with you, staying in perfect oneness with Him.

The life of your Lord is to become your vital, simple life, and the way He worked and lived among people while here on earth must be the way He works and lives in you.

PRAYER IN THE FATHER'S HONOR

". . . that Holy One who is to be born will be called the Son of God"
(LUKE 1:35).

If the Son of God has been born into my human flesh, then am I allowing His holy innocence, simplicity, and oneness with the Father the opportunity to exhibit itself in me? What was true of the Virgin Mary in the history of the Son of God's birth on earth is true of every saint. God's Son is born into me through the direct act of God; then I as His child must exercise the right of a child—the right of always being face to face with my Father through prayer. Do I find myself continually saying in amazement to the common sense part of my life, "Why did you want me to turn here or to go over there? 'Did you not know that I must be about My Father's business?' " (Luke 2:49). Whatever our circumstances may be, that holy, innocent, and eternal Child must be in contact with His Father.

Am I simple enough to identify myself with my Lord in this way? Is He having His wonderful way with me? Is God's will being fulfilled in that His Son has been formed in me (see Galatians 4:19), or have I carefully pushed Him to one side? Oh, the noisy outcry of today! Why does everyone seem to be crying out so loudly? People today are crying out for the Son of God to be put to death. There is no room here for God's Son right now—no room for quiet, holy fellowship and oneness with the Father.

Is the Son of God praying in me, bringing honor to the Father, or am I dictating my demands to Him? Is He ministering in me as He did in the time of His manhood here on earth? Is God's Son in me going through His passion, suffering so that His own purposes might be fulfilled? The more a person knows of the inner life of God's most mature saints, the more he sees what God's purpose really is: to ". . . fill up in my flesh what is lacking in the afflictions of Christ . . ." (Colossians 1:24). And when we think of what it takes to "fill up," there is always something yet to be done.

PRAYER IN THE FATHER'S HEARING

"Jesus lifted up His eyes and said, 'Father, I thank You that You have heard Me' " (JOHN 11:41).

When the Son of God prays, He is mindful and consciously aware of only His Father. God always hears the prayers of His Son, and if the Son of God has been formed in me (see Galatians 4:19) the Father will always hear my prayers. But I must see to it that the Son of God is exhibited in my human flesh. ". . . your body is the temple of the Holy Spirit . . . " (1 Corinthians 6:19), that is, your body is the Bethlehem of God's Son. Is the Son of God being given His opportunity to work in me? Is the direct simplicity of His life being worked out in me exactly as it was worked out in His life while here on earth? When I come into contact with the everyday occurrences of life as an ordinary human being, is the prayer of God's eternal Son to His Father being prayed in me? Jesus says, "In that day you will ask in My name . . ." (John 16:26). What day does He mean? He is referring to the day when the Holy Spirit has come to me and made me one with my Lord.

Is the Lord Jesus Christ being abundantly satisfied by your life, or are you exhibiting a walk of spiritual pride before Him? Never let your common sense become so prominent and forceful that it pushes the Son of God to one side. Common sense is a gift that God gave to our human nature—but common sense is not the gift of His Son. Supernatural sense is the gift of His Son, and we should never put our common sense on the throne. The Son always recognizes and identifies with the Father, but common sense has never yet done so and never will. Our ordinary abilities will never worship God unless they are transformed by the indwelling Son of God. We must make sure that our human flesh is kept in perfect submission to Him, allowing Him to work through it moment by moment. Are we living at such a level of human dependence upon Jesus Christ that His life is being exhibited moment by moment in us?

GOING THROUGH SPIRITUAL CONFUSION

"Jesus answered and said, 'You do not know what you ask' "
(MATTHEW 20:22).

There are times in your spiritual life when there is confusion, and the way out of it is not simply to say that you should not be confused. It is not a matter of right and wrong, but a matter of God taking you through a way that you temporarily do not understand. And it is only by going through the spiritual confusion that you will come to the understanding of what God wants for you.

The Shrouding of His Friendship (see Luke 11:5–8). Jesus gave the illustration here of a man who appears not to care for his friend. He was saying, in effect, that is how the heavenly Father will appear to you at times. You will think that He is an unkind friend, but remember—He is not. The time will come when everything will be explained. There seems to be a cloud on the friendship of the heart, and often even love itself has to wait in pain and tears for the blessing of fuller fellowship and oneness. When God appears to be completely shrouded, will you hang on with confidence in Him?

The Shadow on His Fatherhood (see Luke 11:11–13). Jesus said that there are times when your Father will appear as if He were an unnatural father—as if He were callous and indifferent—but remember, He is not. "Everyone who asks receives..." (Luke 11:10). If all you see is a shadow on the face of the Father right now, hang on to the fact that He will ultimately give you clear understanding and will fully justify Himself in everything that He has allowed into your life.

The Strangeness of His Faithfulness (see Luke 18:1–8). "When the Son of Man comes, will He really find faith on the earth?" (Luke 18:8). Will He find the kind of faith that counts on Him in spite of the confusion? Stand firm in faith, believing that what Jesus said is true, although in the meantime you do not understand what God is doing. He has bigger issues at stake than the particular things you are asking of Him right now.

AFTER SURRENDER—THEN WHAT?

"I have finished the work which You have given Me to do"
(JOHN 17:4).

True surrender is not simply surrender of our external life but surrender of our will—and once that is done, surrender is complete. The greatest crisis we ever face is the surrender of our will. Yet God never forces a person's will into surrender, and He never begs. He patiently waits until that person willingly yields to Him. And once that battle has been fought, it never needs to be fought again.

Surrender for Deliverance. "Come to Me . . . and I will give you rest" (Matthew 11:28). It is only after we have begun to experience what salvation really means that we surrender our will to Jesus for rest. Whatever is causing us a sense of uncertainty is actually a call to our will—"Come to Me." And it is a voluntary coming.

Surrender for Devotion. "If anyone desires to come after Me, let him deny himself..." (Matthew 16:24). The surrender here is of my *self* to Jesus, with His rest at the heart of my being. He says, "If you want to be My disciple, you must give up your right to yourself to Me." And once this is done, the remainder of your life will exhibit nothing but the evidence of this surrender, and you never need to be concerned again with what the future may hold for you. Whatever your circumstances may be, Jesus is totally sufficient (see 2 Corinthians 12:9 and Philippians 4:19).

Surrender for Death. ". . . another will gird you . . ." (John 21:18; also see verse 19). Have you learned what it means to be girded for death? Beware of some surrender that you make to God in an ecstatic moment in your life, because you are apt to take it back again. True surrender is a matter of being "united together [with Jesus] in the likeness of His death" (Romans 6:5) until nothing ever appeals to you that did not appeal to Him.

And after you surrender—then what? Your entire life should be characterized by an eagerness to maintain unbroken fellowship and oneness with God.

ARGUMENTS OR OBEDIENCE?

". . . the simplicity that is in Christ"
(2 CORINTHIANS 11:3).

Simplicity is the secret to seeing things clearly. A saint does not *think* clearly until a long time passes, but a saint ought to *see* clearly without any difficulty. You cannot think through spiritual confusion to make things clear; to make things clear, you must obey. In intellectual matters you can think things out, but in spiritual matters you will only think yourself into further wandering thoughts and more confusion. If there is something in your life upon which God has put His pressure, then obey Him in that matter. Bring all your "arguments and . . . every thought into captivity to the obedience of Christ" regarding the matter, and everything will become as clear as daylight to you (2 Corinthians 10:5). Your reasoning capacity will come later, but reasoning is not how we see. We see like children, and when we try to be wise we see nothing (see Matthew 11:25).

Even the very smallest thing that we allow in our lives that is not under the control of the Holy Spirit is completely sufficient to account for spiritual confusion, and spending all of our time thinking about it will still never make it clear. Spiritual confusion can only be conquered through obedience. As soon as we obey, we have discernment. This is humiliating, because when we are confused we know that the reason lies in the state of our mind. But when our natural power of sight is devoted and submitted in obedience to the Holy Spirit, it becomes the very power by which we perceive God's will, and our entire life is kept in simplicity.

WHAT TO RENOUNCE

"We have renounced the hidden things of shame . . ."
(2 CORINTHIANS 4:2).

Have you "renounced the hidden things of shame" in your life—the things that your sense of honor or pride will not allow to come into the light? You can easily hide them. Is there a thought in your heart about anyone that you would not like to be brought into the light? Then renounce it as soon as it comes to mind—renounce everything in its entirety until there is no hidden dishonesty or craftiness about you at all. Envy, jealousy, and strife don't necessarily arise from your old nature of sin, but from the flesh which was used for these kinds of things in the past (see Romans 6:19 and 1 Peter 4:1–3). You must maintain continual watchfulness so that nothing arises in your life that would cause you shame.

". . . not walking in craftiness. . ." (2 Corinthians 4:2). This means not resorting to something simply to make your own point. This is a terrible trap. You know that God will allow you to work in only one way—the way of truth. Then be careful never to catch people through the other way—the way of deceit. If you act deceitfully, God's blight and ruin will be upon you. What may be craftiness for you, may not be for others—God has called you to a higher standard. Never dull your sense of being your utmost for His highest—your best for His glory. For you, doing certain things would mean craftiness coming into your life for a purpose other than what is the highest and best, and it would dull the motivation that God has given you. Many people have turned back because they are afraid to look at things from God's perspective. The greatest spiritual crisis comes when a person has to move a little farther on in his faith than the beliefs he has already accepted.

PRAYING TO GOD IN SECRET

"When you pray, go into your room, and when you have shut your door, pray to your Father who is in the secret place . . ."
(MATTHEW 6:6).

The primary thought in the area of religion is—keep your eyes on God, not on people. Your motivation should not be the desire to be known as a praying person. Find an inner room in which to pray where no one even knows you are praying, shut the door, and talk to God in secret. Have no motivation other than to know your Father in heaven. It is impossible to carry on your life as a disciple without definite times of secret prayer.

"When you pray, do not use vain repetitions . . ." (6:7). God does not hear us because we pray earnestly— He hears us solely on the basis of redemption. God is never impressed by our earnestness. Prayer is not simply getting things from God—that is only the most elementary kind of prayer. Prayer is coming into perfect fellowship and oneness with God. If the Son of God has been formed in us through regeneration (see Galatians 4:19), then He will continue to press on beyond our common sense and will change our attitude about the things for which we pray.

"Everyone who *asks* receives . . ." (Matthew 7:8). We pray religious nonsense without even involving our will, and then we say that God did not answer—but in reality we have never *asked* for anything. Jesus said, ". . . you will ask what you *desire* . . ." (John 15:7). Asking means that our will must be involved. Whenever Jesus talked about prayer, He spoke with wonderful childlike simplicity. Then we respond with our critical attitude, saying, "Yes, but even Jesus said that we must *ask*." But remember that we have to ask things of God that are in keeping with the God whom Jesus Christ revealed.

IS THERE GOOD IN TEMPTATION?

"No temptation has overtaken you except such as is common to man . . ." (1 CORINTHIANS 10:13).

The word *temptation* has come to mean something bad to us today, but we tend to use the word in the wrong way. Temptation itself is not sin; it is something we are bound to face simply by virtue of being human. Not to be tempted would mean that we were already so shameful that we would be beneath contempt. Yet many of us suffer from temptations we should never have to suffer, simply because we have refused to allow God to lift us to a higher level where we would face temptations of another kind.

A person's inner nature, what he possesses in the inner, spiritual part of his being, determines what he is tempted by on the outside. The temptation fits the true nature of the person being tempted and reveals the possibilities of his nature. Every person actually determines or sets the level of his own temptation, because temptation will come to him in accordance with the level of his controlling, inner nature.

Temptation comes to me, suggesting a possible shortcut to the realization of my highest goal—it does not direct me toward what I understand to be evil, but toward what I understand to be good. Temptation is something that confuses me for a while, and I don't know whether something is right or wrong. When I yield to it, I have made lust a god, and the temptation itself becomes the proof that it was only my own fear that prevented me from falling into the sin earlier.

Temptation is not something we can escape; in fact, it is essential to the well-rounded life of a person. Beware of thinking that you are tempted as no one else—what you go through is the common inheritance of the human race, not something that no one has ever before endured. God does not save us from temptations—He sustains us in the midst of them (see Hebrews 2:18 and 4:15-16).

HIS TEMPTATION AND OURS

**"We do not have a High Priest who cannot sympathize with our
weaknesses, but was in all points tempted as we are, yet without sin"**
(HEBREWS 4:15).

Until we are born again, the only kind of temptation we understand is the kind mentioned in James 1:14, "Each one is tempted
when he is drawn away by his own desires and enticed." But
through regeneration we are lifted into another realm where there are other temptations to face, namely, the kind of temptations our Lord faced.
The temptations of Jesus had no appeal to us as unbelievers because they
were not at home in our human nature. Our Lord's temptations and ours
are in different realms until we are born again and become His brothers.
The temptations of Jesus are not those of a mere man, but the temptations of God as Man. Through regeneration, the Son of God is formed
in us (see Galatians 4:19), and in our physical life He has the same setting
that He had on earth. Satan does not tempt us just to make us do wrong
things—he tempts us to make us lose what God has put into us through
regeneration, namely, the possibility of being of value to God. He does
not come to us on the premise of tempting us to sin, but on the premise
of shifting our point of view, and only the Spirit of God can detect this as
a temptation of the devil.

Temptation means a test of the possessions held within the inner,
spiritual part of our being by a power outside us and foreign to us. This
makes the temptation of our Lord explainable. After Jesus' baptism, having accepted His mission of being the One "who takes away the sin of
the world" (John 1:29) He "was led up by the Spirit into the wilderness"
(Matthew 4:1) and into the testing devices of the devil. Yet He did not
become weary or exhausted. He went through the temptation "without
sin," and He retained all the possessions of His spiritual nature completely intact.

ARE YOU GOING ON WITH JESUS?

"You are those who have continued with Me in My trials"
(LUKE 22:28).

It is true that Jesus Christ is with us through our temptations, but are we going on with Him through His temptations? Many of us turn back from going on with Jesus from the very moment we have an experience of what He can do. Watch when God changes your circumstances to see whether you are going on with Jesus, or siding with the world, the flesh, and the devil. We wear His name, but are we going on with Him? "From that time many of His disciples went back and walked with Him no more" (John 6:66).

The temptations of Jesus continued throughout His earthly life, and they will continue throughout the life of the Son of God in us. Are we going on with Jesus in the life we are living right now?

We have the idea that we ought to shield ourselves from some of the things God brings around us. May it never be! It is God who engineers our circumstances, and whatever they may be we must see that we face them while continually abiding with Him in His temptations. They are *His* temptations, not temptations to us, but temptations to the life of the Son of God in us. Jesus Christ's honor is at stake in our bodily lives. Are we remaining faithful to the Son of God in everything that attacks His life in us?

Are you going on with Jesus? The way goes through Gethsemane, through the city gate, and on "outside the camp" (Hebrews 13:13). The way is lonely and goes on until there is no longer even a trace of a footprint to follow—but only the voice saying, *"Follow Me"* (Matthew 4:19).

THE DIVINE COMMANDMENT OF LIFE

"...be perfect, just as your Father in heaven is perfect" (MATTHEW 5:48).

Our Lord's exhortation to us in verses 38-48 is to be generous in our behavior toward everyone. Beware of living according to your natural affections in your spiritual life. Everyone has natural affections—some people we like and others we don't like. Yet we must never let those likes and dislikes rule our Christian life. "If we walk in the light as He is in the light, we have fellowship with one another" (1 John 1:7), even those toward whom we have no affection.

The example our Lord gave us here is not that of a good person, or even of a good Christian, but of God Himself. "... be perfect, just as your Father in heaven is perfect." In other words, simply show to the other person what God has shown to you. And God will give you plenty of real life opportunities to prove whether or not you are "perfect, just as your Father in heaven is perfect." Being a disciple means deliberately identifying yourself with God's interests in other people. Jesus says, "A new commandment I give to you, that you love one another; as I have loved you, that you also love one another. By this all will know that you are My disciples, if you have love for one another" (John 13:34-35).

The true expression of Christian character is not in good-doing, but in God-likeness. If the Spirit of God has transformed you within, you will exhibit divine characteristics in your life, not just good human characteristics. God's life in us expresses itself as God's life, not as human life trying to be godly. The secret of a Christian's life is that the supernatural becomes natural in him as a result of the grace of God, and the experience of this becomes evident in the practical, everyday details of life, not in times of intimate fellowship with God. And when we come in contact with things that create confusion and a flurry of activity, we find to our own amazement that we have the power to stay wonderfully poised even in the center of it all.

THE "GO" OF PREPARATION

"If you bring your gift to the altar, and there remember that your brother has something against you, leave your gift there before the altar, and go your way. First be reconciled to your brother, and then come and offer your gift"
(MATTHEW 5:23–24).

It is easy for us to imagine that we will suddenly come to a point in our lives where we are fully prepared, but preparation is not suddenly accomplished. In fact, it is a process that must be steadily maintained. It is dangerous to become settled and complacent in our present level of experience. The Christian life requires preparation *and* more preparation.

The sense of sacrifice in the Christian life is readily appealing to a new Christian. From a human standpoint, the one thing that attracts us to Jesus Christ is our sense of the heroic, and a close examination of us by our Lord's words suddenly puts this tide of enthusiasm to the test. "... *go* your way. First be reconciled to your brother. ..." The "go" of preparation is to allow the Word of God to examine you closely. Your sense of heroic sacrifice is not good enough. The thing the Holy Spirit will detect in you is your nature that can never work in His service. And no one but God can detect that nature in you. Do you have anything to hide from God? If you do, then let God search you with His light. If there is sin in your life, don't just *admit* it—*confess* it. Are you willing to obey your Lord and Master, whatever the humiliation to your right to yourself may be?

Never disregard a conviction that the Holy Spirit brings to you. If it is important enough for the Spirit of God to bring it to your mind, it is the very thing He is detecting in you. You were looking for some big thing to give up, while God is telling you of some tiny thing that must go. But behind that tiny thing lies the stronghold of obstinacy, and you say, "I will not give up my right to myself"—the very thing that God intends you to give up if you are to be a disciple of Jesus Christ.

THE "GO" OF RELATIONSHIP

"Whoever compels you to go one mile, go with him two"
(MATTHEW 5:41).

Our Lord's teaching can be summed up in this: the relationship that He demands for us is an impossible one unless He has done a supernatural work in us. Jesus Christ demands that His disciple does not allow even the slightest trace of resentment in his heart when faced with tyranny and injustice. No amount of enthusiasm will ever stand up to the strain that Jesus Christ will put upon His servant. Only one thing will bear the strain, and that is a personal relationship with Jesus Christ Himself—a relationship that has been examined, purified, and tested until only one purpose remains and I can truly say, "I am here for God to send me where He will." Everything else may become blurred, but this relationship with Jesus Christ must never be.

The Sermon on the Mount is not some unattainable goal; it is a statement of what will happen in me when Jesus Christ has changed my nature by putting His own nature in me. Jesus Christ is the only One who can fulfill the Sermon on the Mount.

If we are to be disciples of Jesus, we must be made disciples supernaturally. And as long as we consciously maintain the determined purpose to be His disciples, we can be sure that we are not disciples. Jesus says, "You did not choose Me, but *I chose you* . . ." (John 15:16). That is the way the grace of God begins. It is a constraint we can never escape; we can disobey it, but we can never start it or produce it ourselves. We are drawn to God by a work of His supernatural grace, and we can never trace back to find where the work began. Our Lord's making of a disciple is supernatural. He does not build on any natural capacity of ours at all. God does not ask us to do the things that are naturally easy for us—He only asks us to do the things that we are perfectly fit to do through His grace, and that is where the cross we must bear will always come.

THE "GO" OF RECONCILIATION

"If you ... remember that your brother has something against you ..."
(MATTHEW 5:23).

This verse says, "If you bring your gift to the altar, and there remember that your brother has something against you ...." It is not saying, "If you search and find something because of your unbalanced sensitivity," but, "If you ... remember ...." In other words, if something is brought to your conscious mind by the Spirit of God—"First be reconciled to your brother, and then come and offer your gift" (5:24). Never object to the intense sensitivity of the Spirit of God in you when He is instructing you down to the smallest detail.

"First be reconciled to your brother ...." Our Lord's directive is simple—"First be reconciled ...." He says, in effect, "Go back the way you came—the way indicated to you by the conviction given to you at the altar; have an attitude in your mind and soul toward the person who has something against you that makes reconciliation as natural as breathing." Jesus does not mention the other person—He says for *you* to go. It is not a matter of your rights. The true mark of the saint is that he can waive his own rights and obey the Lord Jesus.

"... and then come and offer your gift." The process of reconciliation is clearly marked. First we have the heroic spirit of self-sacrifice, then the sudden restraint by the sensitivity of the Holy Spirit, and then we are stopped at the point of our conviction. This is followed by obedience to the Word of God, which builds an attitude or state of mind that places no blame on the one with whom you have been in the wrong. And finally there is the glad, simple, unhindered offering of your gift to God.

THE "GO" OF RENUNCIATION

". . . someone said to Him, 'Lord, I will follow You wherever You go' "
(LUKE 9:57).

Our Lord's attitude toward this man was one of severe discouragement, "for He knew what was in man" (John 2:25). We would have said, "I can't imagine why He lost the opportunity of winning that man! Imagine being so cold to him and turning him away so discouraged!" Never apologize for your Lord. The words of the Lord hurt and offend until there is nothing left to be hurt or offended. Jesus Christ had no tenderness whatsoever toward anything that was ultimately going to ruin a person in his service to God. Our Lord's answers were not based on some whim or impulsive thought, but on the knowledge of "what was in man." If the Spirit of God brings to your mind a word of the Lord that hurts you, you can be sure that there is something in you that He wants to hurt to the point of its death.

Luke 9:58. These words destroy the argument of serving Jesus Christ because it is a pleasant thing to do. And the strictness of the rejection that He demands of me allows for nothing to remain in my life but my Lord, myself, and a sense of desperate hope. He says that I must let everyone else come or go, and that I must be guided solely by my relationship to Him. And He says, ". . . the Son of Man has nowhere to lay His head."

Luke 9:59. This man did not want to disappoint Jesus, nor did he want to show a lack of respect for his father. We put our sense of loyalty to our relatives ahead of our loyalty to Jesus Christ, forcing Him to take last place. When your loyalties conflict, always obey Jesus Christ whatever the cost.

Luke 9:61. The person who says, "Lord, I will follow You, but . . .," is the person who is intensely ready to go, but never goes. This man had reservations about going. The exacting call of Jesus has no room for good-byes; good-byes, as we often use them, are pagan, not Christian, because they divert us from the call. Once the call of God comes to you, start going and never stop.

THE "GO" OF UNCONDITIONAL IDENTIFICATION

"Jesus . . . said to him, 'One thing you lack: Go your way, sell whatever you have and give to the poor . . . and come, take up the cross, and follow Me' " (MARK 10:21).

The rich young ruler had the controlling passion to be perfect. When he saw Jesus Christ, he wanted to be like Him. Our Lord never places anyone's personal holiness above everything else when He calls a disciple. Jesus' primary consideration is my absolute annihilation of my right to myself and my identification with Him, which means having a relationship with Him in which there are no other relationships. Luke 14:26 has nothing to do with salvation or sanctification, but deals solely with unconditional identification with Jesus Christ. Very few of us truly know what is meant by the absolute "go" of unconditional identification with, and abandonment and surrender to, Jesus.

"Then Jesus, looking at him, loved him . . ." (Mark 10:21). This look of Jesus will require breaking your heart away forever from allegiance to any other person or thing. Has Jesus ever looked in this way at you? This look of Jesus transforms, penetrates, and captivates. Where you are soft and pliable with God is where the Lord has looked at you. If you are hard and vindictive, insistent on having your own way, and always certain that the other person is more likely to be in the wrong than you are, then there are whole areas of your nature that have never been transformed by His gaze.

"One thing you lack. . . ." From Jesus Christ's perspective, oneness with Him, with nothing between, is the only good thing.

". . . sell whatever you have. . . ." I must humble myself until I am merely a living person. I must essentially renounce possessions of all kinds, not for salvation (for only one thing saves a person and that is absolute reliance in faith upon Jesus Christ), but to follow Jesus. ". . . come . . . and follow Me." And the road is the way He went.

THE AWARENESS OF THE CALL

". . . for necessity is laid upon me; yes, woe is me if I do not preach the gospel!" (1 CORINTHIANS 9:16).

We are inclined to forget the deeply spiritual and supernatural touch of God. If you are able to tell exactly where you were when you received the call of God and can explain all about it, I question whether you have truly been called. The call of God does not come like that; it is much more supernatural. The realization of the call in a person's life may come like a clap of thunder or it may dawn gradually. But however quickly or slowly this awareness comes, it is always accompanied with an undercurrent of the supernatural—something that is inexpressible and produces a "glow." At any moment the sudden awareness of this incalculable, supernatural, surprising call that has taken hold of your life may break through—"I chose you . . ." (John 15:16). The call of God has nothing to do with salvation and sanctification. You are not called to preach the gospel because you are sanctified; the call to preach the gospel is infinitely different. Paul describes it as a compulsion that was placed upon him.

If you have ignored, and thereby removed, the great supernatural call of God in your life, take a review of your circumstances. See where you have put your own ideas of service or your particular abilities ahead of the call of God. Paul said, ". . . woe is me if I do not preach the gospel!" He had become aware of the call of God, and his compulsion to "preach the gospel" was so strong that nothing else was any longer even a competitor for his strength.

If a man or woman is called of God, it doesn't matter how difficult the circumstances may be. God orchestrates every force at work for His purpose in the end. If you will agree with God's purpose, He will bring not only your conscious level but also all the deeper levels of your life, which you yourself cannot reach, into perfect harmony.

THE ASSIGNING OF THE CALL

"I now rejoice in my sufferings for you, and fill up in my flesh what is lacking in the afflictions of Christ, for the sake of His body, which is the church . . ." (COLOSSIANS 1:24).

We take our own spiritual consecration and try to make it into a call of God, but when we get right with Him He brushes all this aside. Then He gives us a tremendous, riveting pain to fasten our attention on something that we never even dreamed could be His call for us. And for one radiant, flashing moment we see His purpose, and we say, "Here am I! Send me" (Isaiah 6:8).

This call has nothing to do with personal sanctification, but with being made broken bread and poured-out wine. Yet God can never make us into wine if we object to the fingers He chooses to use to crush us. We say, "If God would only use His own fingers, and make me broken bread and poured-out wine in a special way, then I wouldn't object!" But when He uses someone we dislike, or some set of circumstances to which we said we would never submit, to crush us, then we object. Yet we must never try to choose the place of our own martyrdom. If we are ever going to be made into wine, we will have to be crushed—you cannot drink grapes. Grapes become wine only when they have been squeezed.

I wonder what finger and thumb God has been using to squeeze you? Have you been as hard as a marble and escaped? If you are not ripe yet, and if God *had* squeezed you anyway, the wine produced would have been remarkably bitter. To be a holy person means that the elements of our natural life experience the very presence of God as they are providentially broken in His service. We have to be placed into God and brought into agreement with Him before we can be broken bread in His hands. Stay right with God and let Him do as He likes, and you will find that He is producing the kind of bread and wine that will benefit His other children.

THE PLACE OF EXALTATION

**"... Jesus took ... them up on a high mountain
apart by themselves ..."** (MARK 9:2).

We have all experienced times of exaltation on the mountain, when we have seen things from God's perspective and have wanted to stay there. But God will never allow us to stay there. The true test of our spiritual life is in exhibiting the power to descend from the mountain. If we only have the power to go up, something is wrong. It is a wonderful thing to be on the mountain with God, but a person only gets there so that he may later go down and lift up the demon-possessed people in the valley (see 9:14–18). We are not made for the mountains, for sunrises, or for the other beautiful attractions in life—those are simply intended to be moments of inspiration. We are made for the valley and the ordinary things of life, and that is where we have to prove our stamina and strength. Yet our spiritual selfishness always wants repeated moments on the mountain. We feel that we could talk and live like perfect angels, if we could only stay on the mountaintop. Those times of exaltation are exceptional and they have their meaning in our life with God, but we must beware to prevent our spiritual selfishness from wanting to make them the only time.

We are inclined to think that everything that happens is to be turned into useful teaching. In actual fact, it is to be turned into something even better than teaching, namely, character. The mountaintop is not meant to *teach* us anything, it is meant to *make* us something. There is a terrible trap in always asking, "What's the use of this experience?" We can never measure spiritual matters in that way. The moments on the mountaintop are rare moments, and they are meant for something in God's purpose.

THE PLACE OF HUMILIATION

"If You can do anything, have compassion on us and help us"
(MARK 9:22).

After every time of exaltation, we are brought down with a sudden rush into things as they really are, where it is neither beautiful, poetic, nor thrilling. The height of the mountaintop is measured by the dismal drudgery of the valley, but it is in the valley that we have to live for the glory of God. We *see* His glory on the mountain, but we never *live* for His glory there. It is in the place of humiliation that we find our true worth to God—that is where our faithfulness is revealed. Most of us can do things if we are always at some heroic level of intensity, simply because of the natural selfishness of our own hearts. But God wants us to be at the drab everyday level, where we live in the valley according to our personal relationship with Him. Peter thought it would be a wonderful thing for them to remain on the mountain, but Jesus Christ took the disciples down from the mountain and into the valley, where the true meaning of the vision was explained (see 9:5-6, 14-23).

"If you can do anything...." It takes the valley of humiliation to remove the skepticism from us. Look back at your own experience and you will find that until you learned who Jesus really was, you were a skillful skeptic about His power. When you were on the mountaintop you could believe anything, but what about when you were faced with the facts of the valley? You may be able to give a testimony regarding your sanctification, but what about the thing that is a humiliation to you right now? The last time you were on the mountain with God, you saw that all the power in heaven and on earth belonged to Jesus—will you be skeptical now, simply because you are in the valley of humiliation?

THE PLACE OF MINISTRY

"He said to them, 'This kind [of unclean spirit] can come out by nothing but prayer and fasting' " (MARK 9:29).

H is disciples asked Him privately, 'Why could we not cast it out?' " (9:28). The answer lies in a personal relationship with Jesus Christ. "This kind can come out by nothing but" concentrating on Him, and then doubling and redoubling that concentration on Him. We can remain powerless forever, as the disciples were in this situation, by trying to do God's work without concentrating on His power, and by following instead the ideas that we draw from our own nature. We actually slander and dishonor God by our very eagerness to serve Him without knowing Him.

When you are brought face to face with a difficult situation and nothing happens externally, you can still know that freedom and release will be given because of your continued concentration on Jesus Christ. Your duty in service and ministry is to see that there is nothing between Jesus and yourself. Is there anything between you and Jesus even now? If there is, you must get through it, not by ignoring it as an irritation, or by going up and over it, but by facing it and getting through it into the presence of Jesus Christ. Then that very problem itself, and all that you have been through in connection with it, will glorify Jesus Christ in a way that you will never know until you see Him face to face.

We must be able to "mount up with wings like eagles" (Isaiah 40:31), but we must also know how to come down. The power of the saint lies in the coming down and in the living that is done in the valley. Paul said, "I can do all things through Christ who strengthens me" (Philippians 4:13) and what he was referring to were mostly humiliating things. And yet it is in our power to refuse to be humiliated and to say, "No, thank you, I much prefer to be on the mountaintop with God." Can I face things as they actually are in the light of the reality of Jesus Christ, or do things as they really are destroy my faith in Him, and put me into a panic?

THE VISION AND THE REALITY

". . . to those who are . . . called to be saints . . ."
(1 CORINTHIANS 1:2).

Thank God for being able to see all that you have not yet been. You have had the vision, but you are not yet to the reality of it by any means. It is when we are in the valley, where we prove whether we will be the choice ones, that most of us turn back. We are not quite prepared for the bumps and bruises that must come if we are going to be turned into the shape of the vision. We have seen what we are not, and what God wants us to be, but are we willing to be battered into the shape of the vision to be used by God? The beatings will always come in the most common, everyday ways and through common, everyday people.

There are times when we do know what God's purpose is; whether we will let the vision be turned into actual character depends on us, not on God. If we prefer to relax on the mountaintop and live in the memory of the vision, then we will be of no real use in the ordinary things of which human life is made. We have to learn to live in reliance upon what we saw in the vision, not simply live in ecstatic delight and conscious reflection upon God. This means living the realities of our lives in the light of the vision until the truth of the vision is actually realized in us. Every bit of our training is in that direction. Learn to thank God for making His demands known.

Our little "I am" always sulks and pouts when God says *do*. Let your little "I am" be shriveled up in God's wrath and indignation—"I AM WHO I AM . . . has sent me to you" (Exodus 3:14). He must dominate. Isn't it piercing to realize that God not only knows where we live, but also knows the gutters into which we crawl! He will hunt us down as fast as a flash of lightning. No human being knows human beings as God does.

THE UNHEEDED SECRET

"Jesus answered, 'My kingdom is not of this world' "
(JOHN 18:36).

The great enemy of the Lord Jesus Christ today is the idea of practical work that has no basis in the New Testament but comes from the systems of the world. This work insists upon endless energy and activities, but no private life with God. The emphasis is put on the wrong thing. Jesus said, "The kingdom of God does not come with observation . . . . For indeed, the kingdom of God is within you" (Luke 17:20–21). It is a hidden, obscure thing. An active Christian worker too often lives to be seen by others, while it is the innermost, personal area that reveals the power of a person's life.

We must get rid of the plague of the spirit of this religious age in which we live. In our Lord's life there was none of the pressure and the rushing of tremendous activity that we regard so highly today, and a disciple is to be like His Master. The central point of the kingdom of Jesus Christ is a personal relationship with Him, not public usefulness to others.

It is not the practical activities that are the strength of this Bible Training College—its entire strength lies in the fact that here you are immersed in the truths of God to soak in them before Him. You have no idea of where or how God is going to engineer your future circumstances, and no knowledge of what stress and strain is going to be placed on you either at home or abroad. And if you waste your time in overactivity, instead of being immersed in the great fundamental truths of God's redemption, then you will snap when the stress and strain do come. But if this time of soaking before God is being spent in getting rooted and grounded in Him, which may appear to be impractical, then you will remain true to Him whatever happens.

IS GOD'S WILL MY WILL?

"This is the will of God, your sanctification . . ."
(1 THESSALONIANS 4:3).

Sanctification is not a question of whether God is willing to sanctify me—is it *my* will? Am I willing to let God do in me everything that has been made possible through the atonement of the Cross of Christ? Am I willing to let Jesus become sanctification to me, and to let His life be exhibited in my human flesh? (see 1 Corinthians 1:30). Beware of saying, "Oh, I am longing to be sanctified." No, you are not. Recognize your need, but stop longing and make it a matter of action. Receive Jesus Christ to become sanctification for you by absolute, un-questioning faith, and the great miracle of the atonement of Jesus will become real in you.

All that Jesus made possible becomes mine through the free and loving gift of God on the basis of what Christ accomplished on the cross. And my attitude as a saved and sanctified soul is that of profound, humble holiness (there is no such thing as proud holiness). It is a holiness based on agonizing repentance, a sense of inexpressible shame and degradation, and also on the amazing realization that the love of God demonstrated itself to me while I cared nothing about Him (see Romans 5:8). He completed everything for my salvation and sanctification. No wonder Paul said that nothing "shall be able to separate us from the love of God which is in Christ Jesus our Lord" (Romans 8:39).

Sanctification makes me one with Jesus Christ, and in Him one with God, and it is accomplished only through the magnificent atonement of Christ. Never confuse the effect with the cause. The effect in me is obedi-ence, service, and prayer, and is the outcome of inexpressible thanks and adoration for the miraculous sanctification that has been brought about in me because of the atonement through the Cross of Christ.

IMPULSIVENESS OR DISCIPLESHIP?

**"But you, beloved, building yourselves up on
your most holy faith . . ."** (JUDE 20).

There was nothing of the nature of impulsive or thoughtless action about our Lord, but only a calm strength that never got into a panic. Most of us develop our Christianity along the lines of our own nature, not along the lines of God's nature. Impulsiveness is a trait of the natural life, and our Lord always ignores it, because it hinders the development of the life of a disciple. Watch how the Spirit of God gives a sense of restraint to impulsiveness, suddenly bringing us a feeling of self-conscious foolishness, which makes us instantly want to vindicate ourselves. Impulsiveness is all right in a child, but is disastrous in a man or woman—an impulsive adult is always a spoiled person. Impulsiveness needs to be trained into intuition through discipline.

Discipleship is built entirely on the supernatural grace of God. Walking on water is easy to someone with impulsive boldness, but walking on dry land as a disciple of Jesus Christ is something altogether different. Peter walked on the water to go to Jesus, but he "followed Him at a distance" on dry land (Mark 14:54). We do not need the grace of God to withstand crises—human nature and pride are sufficient for us to face the stress and strain magnificently. But it does require the supernatural grace of God to live twenty-four hours of every day as a saint, going through drudgery, and living an ordinary, unnoticed, and ignored existence as a disciple of Jesus. It is ingrained in us that we have to do exceptional things for God—but we do not. We have to be exceptional in the ordinary things of life, and holy on the ordinary streets, among ordinary people—and this is not learned in five minutes.

THE WITNESS OF THE SPIRIT

"The Spirit Himself bears witness with our spirit . . ."
(ROMANS 8:16).

We are in danger of getting into a bargaining spirit with God when we come to Him—we want the witness of the Spirit before we have done what God tells us to do.

Why doesn't God reveal Himself to you? He cannot. It is not that He will not, but He cannot, because you are in the way as long as you won't abandon yourself to Him in total surrender. Yet once you do, immediately God witnesses to Himself—He cannot witness to you, but He instantly witnesses to His own nature in you. If you received the witness of the Spirit before the reality and truth that comes from obedience, it would simply result in sentimental emotion. But when you act on the basis of redemption, and stop the disrespectfulness of debating with God, He immediately gives His witness. As soon as you abandon your own reasoning and arguing, God witnesses to what He has done, and you are amazed at your total disrespect in having kept Him waiting. If you are debating as to whether or not God can deliver from sin, then either let Him do it or tell Him that He cannot. Do not quote this or that person to Him. Simply obey Matthew 11:28, "Come to Me, all you who labor and are heavy laden . . . ." *Come,* if you are weary, and *ask,* if you know you are evil (see Luke 11:9–13).

The Spirit of God witnesses to the redemption of our Lord, and to nothing else. He cannot witness to our reason. We are inclined to mistake the simplicity that comes from our natural common-sense decisions for the witness of the Spirit, but the Spirit witnesses only to His own nature, and to the work of redemption, never to our reason. If we are trying to make Him witness to our reason, it is no wonder that we are in darkness and uncertainty. Throw it all overboard, trust in Him, and He will give you the witness of the Spirit.

NOTHING OF THE OLD LIFE!

"If anyone is in Christ, he is a new creation; old things have passed away; behold, all things have become new"
(2 CORINTHIANS 5:17).

Our Lord never tolerates our prejudices—He is directly opposed to them and puts them to death. We tend to think that God has some special interest in our particular prejudices, and are very sure that He will never deal with us as He has to deal with others. We even say to ourselves, "God has to deal with other people in a very strict way, but of course He knows that my prejudices are all right." But we must learn that God accepts nothing of the old life! Instead of being on the side of our prejudices, He is deliberately removing them from us. It is part of our moral education to see our prejudices put to death by His providence, and to watch how He does it. God pays no respect to anything we bring to Him. There is only one thing God wants of us, and that is our unconditional surrender.

When we are born again, the Holy Spirit begins to work His new creation in us, and there will come a time when there is nothing remaining of the old life. Our old gloomy outlook disappears, as does our old attitude toward things, and "all things are of God" (5:18). How are we going to get a life that has no lust, no self-interest, and is not sensitive to the ridicule of others? How will we have the type of love that "is kind . . . is not provoked, [and] thinks no evil"? (1 Corinthians 13:4–5). The only way is by allowing nothing of the old life to remain, and by having only simple, perfect trust in God—such a trust that we no longer want God's blessings, but only want God Himself. Have we come to the point where God can withdraw His blessings from us without our trust in Him being affected? Once we truly see God at work, we will never be concerned again about the things that happen, because we are actually trusting in our Father in heaven, whom the world cannot see.

THE PROPER PERSPECTIVE

"Thanks be to God who always leads us in triumph in Christ . . ."
(2 CORINTHIANS 2:14).

The proper perspective of a servant of God must not simply be as near to the highest as he can get, but it must be *the* highest. Be careful that you vigorously maintain God's perspective, and remember that it must be done every day, little by little. Don't think on a finite level. No outside power can touch the proper perspective.

The proper perspective to maintain is that we are here for only one purpose—to be captives marching in the procession of Christ's triumphs. We are not on display in God's showcase—we are here to exhibit only one thing—the "captivity [of our lives] to the obedience of Christ" (2 Corinthians 10:5). How small all the other perspectives are! For example, the ones that say, "I am standing all alone, battling for Jesus," or, "I have to maintain the cause of Christ and hold down this fort for Him." But Paul said, in essence, "I am in the procession of a conqueror, and it doesn't matter what the difficulties are, for I am always led in triumph." Is this idea being worked out practically in us? Paul's secret joy was that God took him as a blatant rebel against Jesus Christ, and made him a captive—and that became his purpose. It was Paul's joy to be a captive of the Lord, and he had no other interest in heaven or on earth. It is a shameful thing for a Christian to talk about getting the victory. We should belong so completely to the Victor that it is always His victory, and "we are more than conquerors through Him . . ." (Romans 8:37).

"We are to God the fragrance of Christ . . ." (2 Corinthians 2:15). We are encompassed with the sweet aroma of Jesus, and wherever we go we are a wonderful refreshment to God.

SUBMITTING TO GOD'S PURPOSE

"I have become all things to all men, that I might by all means save some" (1 CORINTHIANS 9:22).

A Christian worker has to learn how to be God's man or woman of great worth and excellence in the midst of a multitude of meager and worthless things. Never protest by saying, "If only I were somewhere else!" All of God's people are ordinary people who have been made extraordinary by the purpose He has given them. Unless we have the right purpose intellectually in our minds and lovingly in our hearts, we will very quickly be diverted from being useful to God. We are not workers for God by choice. Many people deliberately choose to be workers, but they have no purpose of God's almighty grace or His mighty Word in them. Paul's whole heart, mind, and soul were consumed with the great purpose of what Jesus Christ came to do, and he never lost sight of that one thing. We must continually confront ourselves with one central fact—". . . Jesus Christ and Him crucified" (1 Corinthians 2:2).

"I chose you . . ." (John 15:16). Keep these words as a wonderful reminder in your theology. It is not that you have gotten God, but that He has gotten you. God is at work bending, breaking, molding, and doing exactly as He chooses. And why is He doing it? He is doing it for only one purpose—that He may be able to say, "This is My man, and this is My woman." We have to be in God's hand so that He can place others on the Rock, Jesus Christ, just as He has placed us.

Never choose to be a worker, but once God has placed His call upon you, woe be to you if you "turn aside . . . to the right or the left . . ." (Deuteronomy 28:14). He will do with you what He never did before His call came to you, and He will do with you what He is not doing with other people. Let Him have His way.

WHAT IS A MISSIONARY?

"Jesus said to them again, '. . . As the Father has sent Me, I also send you' " (JOHN 20:21).

A missionary is someone sent by Jesus Christ just as He was sent by God. The great controlling factor is not the needs of people, but the command of Jesus. The source of our inspiration in our service for God is behind us, not ahead of us. The tendency today is to put the inspiration out in front—to sweep everything together in front of us and make it conform to our definition of success. But in the New Testament the inspiration is put behind us, and is the Lord Jesus Himself. The goal is to be true to Him—to carry out *His* plans.

Personal attachment to the Lord Jesus and to His perspective is the one thing that must not be overlooked. In missionary work the great danger is that God's call will be replaced by the needs of the people, to the point that human sympathy for those needs will absolutely overwhelm the meaning of being sent by Jesus. The needs are so enormous, and the conditions so difficult, that every power of the mind falters and fails. We tend to forget that the one great reason underneath all missionary work is not primarily the elevation of the people, their education, nor their needs, but is first and foremost the command of Jesus Christ—"Go therefore and make disciples of all the nations . . ." (Matthew 28:19).

When looking back on the lives of men and women of God, the tendency is to say, "What wonderfully keen and intelligent wisdom they had, and how perfectly they understood all that God wanted!" But the keen and intelligent mind behind them was the mind of God, not human wisdom at all. We give credit to human wisdom when we should give credit to the divine guidance of God being exhibited through childlike people who were "foolish" enough to trust God's wisdom and His supernatural equipment.

THE METHOD OF MISSIONS

"Go therefore and make disciples of all the nations..."
(MATTHEW 28:19).

Jesus Christ did not say, "Go and save souls" (the salvation of souls is the supernatural work of God), but He said, "Go ... make disciples of all the nations ...." Yet you cannot make disciples unless you are a disciple yourself. When the disciples returned from their first mission, they were filled with joy because even the demons were subject to them. But Jesus said, in effect, "Don't rejoice in successful service—the great secret of joy is that you have the right relationship with Me" (see Luke 10:17-20). The missionary's great essential is remaining true to the call of God, and realizing that his one and only purpose is to disciple men and women to Jesus. Remember that there is a passion for souls that does not come from God, but from our desire to make converts to our point of view.

The challenge to the missionary does not come from the fact that people are difficult to bring to salvation, that backsliders are difficult to reclaim, or that there is a barrier of callous indifference. No, the challenge comes from the perspective of the missionary's own personal relationship with Jesus Christ—"Do you believe that I am able to do this?" (Matthew 9:28). Our Lord unwaveringly asks us that question, and it confronts us in every individual situation we encounter. The one great challenge to us is—do I know my risen Lord? Do I know the power of His indwelling Spirit? Am I wise enough in God's sight, but foolish enough according to the wisdom of the world, to trust in what Jesus Christ has said? Or am I abandoning the great supernatural position of limitless confidence in Christ Jesus, which is really God's only call for a missionary? If I follow any other method, I depart altogether from the methods prescribed by our Lord—"All authority has been given to Me .... Go *therefore* ..." (Matthew 28:18-19).

JUSTIFICATION BY FAITH

"If when we were enemies we were reconciled to God through the death of His Son, much more, having been reconciled, we shall be saved by His life"
(ROMANS 5:10).

I am not saved by believing—I simply realize I am saved by believing. And it is not repentance that saves me— repentance is only the sign that I realize what God has done through Christ Jesus. The danger here is putting the emphasis on the effect, instead of on the cause. Is it my obedience, consecration, and dedication that make me right with God? It is never that! I am made right with God because, prior to all of that, Christ died. When I turn to God and by belief accept what God reveals, the miraculous atonement by the Cross of Christ instantly places me into a right relationship with God. And as a result of the supernatural miracle of God's grace I stand justified, not because I am sorry for my sin, or because I have repented, but because of what Jesus has done. The Spirit of God brings justification with a shattering, radiant light, and I know that I am saved, even though I don't know how it was accomplished.

The salvation that comes from God is not based on human logic, but on the sacrificial death of Jesus. We can be born again solely because of the atonement of our Lord. Sinful men and women can be changed into new creations, not through their repentance or their belief, but through the wonderful work of God in Christ Jesus which preceded all of our experience (see 2 Corinthians 5:17–19). The unconquerable safety of justification and sanctification is God Himself. We do not have to accomplish these things ourselves—they have been accomplished through the atonement of the Cross of Christ. The supernatural becomes natural to us through the miracle of God, and there is the realization of what Jesus Christ has already done—"*It is finished!*" (John 19:30).

SUBSTITUTION

"He made Him who knew no sin to be sin for us, that we might become the righteousness of God in Him"
(2 CORINTHIANS 5:21).

The modern view of the death of Jesus is that He died for our sins out of sympathy for us. Yet the New Testament view is that He took our sin on Himself not because of sympathy, but because of His identification with us. He was *"made . . . to be sin . . . ."* Our sins are removed because of the death of Jesus, and the only explanation for His death is His obedience to His Father, not His sympathy for us. We are acceptable to God not because we have obeyed, nor because we have promised to give up things, but because of the death of Christ, and for no other reason. We say that Jesus Christ came to reveal the fatherhood and the lovingkindness of God, but the New Testament says that He came to take "away the sin of the world!" (John 1:29). And the revealing of the fatherhood of God is only to those to whom Jesus has been introduced as Savior. In speaking to the world, Jesus Christ never referred to Himself as One who revealed the Father, but He spoke instead of being a stumbling block (see John 15:22-24). John 14:9, where Jesus said, "He who has seen Me has seen the Father," was spoken to His disciples.

That Christ died for me, and therefore I am completely free from penalty, is never taught in the New Testament. What *is* taught in the New Testament is that "He died for all" (2 Corinthians 5:15)—not, "He died my death"—and that through identification with His death I can be freed from sin, and have His very righteousness imparted as a gift to me. The substitution which is taught in the New Testament is twofold—"For He made Him who knew no sin to be sin for us, *that we might become the righteousness of God in Him."* The teaching is not Christ *for* me unless I am determined to have Christ formed *in* me (see Galatians 4:19).

FAITH

"Without faith it is impossible to please Him . . ."
(HEBREWS 11:6).

Faith in active opposition to common sense is mistaken enthusiasm and narrow-mindedness, and common sense in opposition to faith demonstrates a mistaken reliance on reason as the basis for truth. The life of faith brings the two of these into the proper relationship. Common sense and faith are as different from each other as the natural life is from the spiritual, and as impulsiveness is from inspiration. Nothing that Jesus Christ ever said is common sense, but is revelation sense, and is complete, whereas common sense falls short. Yet faith must be tested and tried before it becomes real in your life. "We know that all things work together for good . . ." (Romans 8:28) so that no matter what happens, the transforming power of God's providence transforms perfect faith into reality. Faith always works in a personal way, because the purpose of God is to see that perfect faith is made real in His children.

For every detail of common sense in life, there is a truth God has revealed by which we can prove in our practical experience what we believe God to be. Faith is a tremendously active principle that always puts Jesus Christ first. The life of faith says, "Lord, You have said it, it appears to be irrational, but I'm going to step out boldly, trusting in Your Word" (for example, see Matthew 6:33). Turning intellectual faith into our personal possession is *always* a fight, not just sometimes. God brings us into particular circumstances to educate our faith, because the nature of faith is to make the object of our faith very real to us. Until we know Jesus, God is merely a concept, and we can't have faith in Him. But once we hear Jesus say, "He who has seen Me has seen the Father" (John 14:9) we immediately have something that is real, and our faith is limitless. Faith is the entire person in the right relationship with God through the power of the Spirit of Jesus Christ.

Scripture Index

ALL OF OSWALD CHAMBERS' WRITINGS IN ONE VOLUME

The Complete Works of Oswald Chambers

Now you can own all of Oswald Chambers' books, including the devotional *My Utmost for His Highest,* and two never-before-printed studies in one complete volume. This hardbound, 1,512-page compilation also includes insightful notes by author and Chambers biographer David McCasland and a fully searchable CD-ROM* containing the entire volume.

　　You are sure to find this complete work a timeless treasure that you can enjoy again and again.

The Complete Works of Oswald Chambers includes:

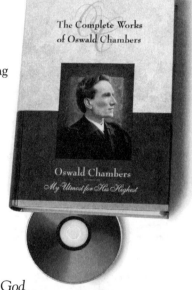

- All 34 of Chambers' works, including *My Utmost for His Highest*

- Never-before-published study notes on Isaiah and Jeremiah

- Insightful notes on Oswald Chambers by biographer David McCasland

- A fully searchable CD-ROM* also includes the autobiography, *Oswald Chambers: Abandoned to God*

#RFMU-039X, 1,512-page hardcover with CD-ROM
Regularly $40.95, only $36.85*

*Requires Windows® XP or later.

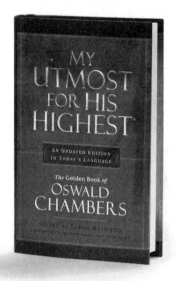

MORE WORKS FROM OSWALD CHAMBERS

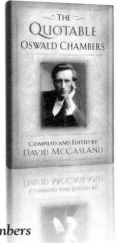
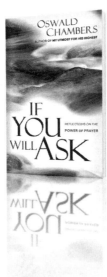

Available wherever books are sold. To order online, visit
www.dhp.org, or call Discovery House Publishers at:
1-800-653-8333

NOTES

NOTES

NOTES

NOTES

NOTES

NOTES

NOTES

NOTES

NOTES